Behind Good and Evil

How to Overcome the Death-Dealing
Character of Morality

Scott W. Gustafson

Copyright © 2009 by Scott W. Gustafson

ISBN 0-7414-5404-1

Biblical quotations are from the Revised Standard Version of the Bible, copyright 1952 (2nd edition, 1971) by the Division of Christian Education of the National Council of Churches of Christ in the United States of America. Used by permission. All rights reserved.

Published by:

PUBLISHING.COM

1094 New DeHaven Street, Suite 100
West Conshohocken, PA 19428-2713
Info@buybooksontheweb.com
www.buybooksontheweb.com
Toll-free (877) BUY BOOK
Local Phone (610) 941-9999
Fax (610) 941-9959

Printed in the United States of America

Published July 2009

For the good people of the world

Table of Contents

Preface

President Woodrow Wilson called World War I the war to end all wars. Sadly, he was wrong. In the century following that war, more people have been violently killed than in any other century in history, and most killings were caused or justified by our moral precepts. This century is likely to bring even more avoidable death and carnage. Rapid climate change will produce enormous inequalities which will increase the chances of even more violent conflicts. If our past is any indication of our future, the haves will find morally satisfying justifications for their good fortune, and the resentment of the have-nots will grow. No doubt the have-nots will also develop morally satisfying reasons to lash out against those who defend and violently enforce rules that justify inequalities under which others suffer. Popular belief often asserts that the absence of morality leads to violence and death, and, in accord with popular will, our leaders suggest moral solutions for our problems. The fact is, however, that morality itself may be the problem.

Life-giving change requires a sober assessment of morality which is described in this book as our knowledge of good and evil. Morality is not a remedy for that which ails us. It is actually the problem. The first part of this book, specifically Chapters 2-4, discloses morality's death-dealing characteristics. The last chapters propose an alternative way to think and live. This way is a path to peace. It is naturally human. It is embedded in the foundations of nearly every religion in the world. It offers the possibility of imagining a future built on the affirmation of life instead of death. This alternative is called ethics.

Riane Eisler's book *The Chalice and the Blade* provides the framework of analysis behind this work. She distinguishes between two ways of living and ordering life she calls the dominator and partnership model. Morality – our knowledge of good and evil – is reasoned human behavior that supports the dominator model. Ethics is reasoned human behavior that supports the partnership model. This is the simplest way to explain this book's rather unusual assertion that ethics is different from morality. While others have distinguished between morality and ethics, the distinction made here is more closely aligned with Latin American liberation theologian Enrique Dussell's book *Ethics and Community*. In this book Dussell contends that morality justifies and sanctifies political and economic regimes from monarchy to democracy and from capitalism to socialism. In contrast, ethics concerns the needs of those who these systems have marginalized.

Daniel Quinn and Neil Postman also give direction to this inquiry. Quinn appreciates the fact that humanity's existence predates the origin of what we know as civilization by at least 150,000 years. He also recognizes that the agricultural revolution was not the purely positive thing that we often take it to be. Indeed, it set forces in motion that could lead to the demise of the human race if we are not careful. Postman's contention that technology is never socially or ideologically neutral helps account for the forces Quinn thinks the agricultural revolution set in motion.

Zygmunt Bauman's book *Modernity and the Holocaust* extends the observations made concerning the power implicit in the agricultural revolution's technology. This book cogently argues that the Holocaust was not simply a moral malfunction. Instead the Holocaust is consistent with morality and civilization. (I know this assertion sounds strange to civilized ears. Chapters 2-4, however, make this strange claim plausible). My son Gregory Gustafson reinforced this argument for me by informing me of the overtly racist claims of some of the Western world's great philosophers. Upon reading the racist accounts of philosophical giants like John Locke, David Hume, Immanuel Kant, George F.W. Hegel, Thomas Jefferson and others, one must pause and recognize how deeply engrained racism is in Western civilization. Racism, like the Holocaust, is not the moral defect we often suppose it to be. It too is consistent with morality (as morality will soon be described) and with the principles of Western civilization.

Darrell Fasching and Del Dechant's systematic distinction between the sacred and the Holy allowed me to see that a moral person focuses on what his or her culture deems sacred while the ethical person challenges the very things his or her culture deems sacred, and does so in the name of the Holy. Perhaps of even more importance, however, is that their work helped me clarify what I am doing here. In their book *Comparative Religious Ethics* and in Fasching's *The Ethical Challenge of Auschwitz and Hiroshima* the story of how the Christian Tolstoy changed his understanding of Christianity after reading a Christianized version of the Hindu story *Bhagavad Gita.* Tolstoy's new understanding of Christianity influenced the Hindu Gandhi who, in turn, influenced the Christian Martin Luther King Jr. Fasching and Delchant call this cross pollination of the religious traditions "crossing over."

This book is my feeble attempt to cross over to certain American Indian religions and spiritualities. I have done this by reading alone. I do not seek to participate in their actual spiritual practices for two reasons. First, they are too demanding and I don't think I could physically or spiritually do it!! Second, my readings inform me that white participation results in stealing the American Indian spirit as we have stolen their land. We have already stolen enough from the American Indians, so I listen from a distance. I read works they are kind enough to publish, and what they have published both exposes the fundamental unfaithfulness of my Christian tradition to Jesus, and gives me hope that maybe repentance and life are still possible. The seminal writings of Vine Deloria Jr. are of profound significance, but of at least as much significance to me is the work of George E. Tinker. His books *Spirit and Resistance* and *Missionary Conquest* should be read by every Christian who is, as the prophet says, "at ease in Zion."

Many friends and colleagues have read this manuscript and made very helpful comments. Mark Zimmerman is one of my oldest friends. While we were barely teenagers, Mark instilled in me a love of reading. I do not think I would have read a book outside of school without his encouragement. He made some very helpful suggestions in the early stages of this book. Don Wilcox and Bill Doran –two of my friends and colleagues – also helped me with this book. Don helped me clarify my definition of civilization and Bill, who read the manuscript at a much later stage, made suggestions that made the text easier to read. Bill greatly encouraged me when he said that many parts were "lucid." Those who know Bill know he more frequently uses the word obtuse than lucid. My friend, former student and colleague, Bélen González y Pérez also made some important suggestions to this book, but of most importance to me is the compassion and care with which he read the manuscript. He possesses the ability to understand things from a perspective that sheds light on my own unconscious prejudices. I know that he could not possibly eliminate all of them in this manuscript, but he has illuminated and eliminated many. Philip Brenner contributed a perspective that this book would lack if he had not been so kind in his help. I gave him the manuscript to read when it was about 80% complete. (I only knew it was 80% complete after he read it!!). His many cogent suggestions brought the project to completion (if we ever actually complete anything). I fail to see how this book would be half as good as it now is without his assistance. Words cannot express my gratitude to these people who took time out of their lives to read what I have written. They all honored me with their attention. They did this out of friendship and I deeply appreciate their assistance and, more importantly, their friendship. My sister, Paula Gustafson, designed the cover of this book. Among her many talents is the ability to visually express concepts. I suppose I should also thank our parents for giving me such a generous and talented sister. Finally, my wife Brenda Lange-Gustafson has always helped me with my writing. She challenges my concepts and makes my expressions far more clear than they would otherwise be. She does this and many other far more important things out of love, and I am in awe of her continued support.

"Why do you call me good?"

Jesus of Nazareth

Mark 10: 18

Introduction

> "Comprehension . . . means the unpremeditated attentive facing up to, and resisting reality – whatever (reality) may be."
>
> Hannah Arendt[1]

The conflict between good and evil presides over our reflection. It is the background against which great literature is written. It creates the drama in many popular films. It governs our understanding of world events. While sworn enemies like Osama bin Laden and George Bush disagree about who is good and who represents evil, they clearly agree that the struggle in which they are engaged is an eternal struggle between the forces of good and the forces of evil.

Christianity often supports this dangerous belief. C.S. Lewis' children's book *The Lion, The Witch, and The Wardrobe* is hauntingly illustrative.[2] This story is cast using the conflict between good and evil as its background. It ends with the Christ figure, the lion Aslan, substituting himself for the 'sinner' Edmund. Like Jesus, Aslan dies to save the life of the sinner. Like Jesus, Aslan rises from death. *Unlike* Jesus, Aslan leads the forces of good to victory over forces of evil. Good defeats evil only because the good guys are better at employing the same methods that the evil ones employ. The objective of both sides is the same: kill the enemy. It often goes unnoticed, but Christ figures like Aslan do not actually mimic Jesus. Jesus never returned evil for evil. Jesus forgave his executioners, and Jesus did not lead the forces of good in the slaughter of the forces of evil. Jesus supported life instead. His concern was the life of his friends and enemies alike.

This book challenges the notion that morality - our knowledge of good and evil - is life affirming. Not only does it argue that the so-called struggle between good and evil is death-dealing, this presentation suggests that morality has a universal function in all civilizations that promotes social marginalization and death. A different approach to human behavior called ethics is contrasted with morality in this book. Ethics and morality differ because they support different worldviews.

Morality is reasoned human behavior that serves civilization and orders society consistent with a worldview the first chapter describes as the dominator system. Ethics is reasoned human behavior that serves life and orders society consistent with partnership ways. Since morality serves civilization and ethics serves partnership, moral thoughts and actions are different from ethical thoughts and actions. In order to understand the story this book tries to tell, it is necessary to remember that morality and ethics support two quite different worldviews. While a full description of the dominator system and partnership ways will be postponed until the first chapter, some preliminary remarks might be helpful.

Morality serves civilization by distinguishing between good and evil. It declares who or what is good. It pronounces who or what is evil. Since civilizations, communities, religions and individuals usually differ about what constitutes good and evil, the content of morality differs from place to place. Sadly, these opposing moral claims justify much carnage. Indeed, one reason a state of war exists between people Americans call "militant Islamic extremists" and the United States of America is that each warring group understands good and evil differently. Their respective views of good and evil allow the "Islamic extremists" to believe America is evil and Americans to think the extremists are evil. Even though each civilization disagrees about the nature of good and evil, both are moral because *distinguishing between good and evil is morality's most fundamental act.* In other words, morality exists whenever a divide is drawn between the "good" ones and the "evil" ones. The fact that such distinctions are made throughout civilization indicates the scope of our predicament.

Morality usually justifies the general direction in which a particular civilization is already moving. More often than not, the victorious civilization or group determines the nature of good and evil and justifies inequalities with their moral code. For example, the Puritans and Pilgrims often justified their near genocidal treatment of the Native American population with the belief that they (the Puritans) were the chosen people of God. They believed they were like the Israelites who conquered Canaan; hence, they had a God-given right to conquer the New World. In most cases, moral reasoning posits innate differences in race, intelligence or divine favor that enable the dominant group to be victorious over the subordinate group. Indeed, Chapter 3 argues that this sort of reasoning was an important component of the thinking of many great Western philosophers whose philosophy tended to elevate Europeans over other human beings and justify Western civilization's racism.

Jared Diamond's book *Guns, Germs and Steel: The Fates of Human Societies* challenges such moral justifications of social inequalities.[3] Instead, he argues that non-human factors like geography or the natural distribution of certain plants and animals created human inequalities. In other words, social inequalities are based on external environmental factors rather than internal qualities like superior intelligence or racial characteristics.

Diamond realizes that farmers had an obvious cultural advantage over hunter-gatherers. First, their sedentary life styles enable them to acquire excess food and possessions. (The possessions of hunter-gatherers are limited to what can be carried in one's arms from place to place. The farmer can acquire more possessions because the farmer can store them). Second, excess food makes larger and denser population centers possible. Third, the cross pollination of ideas in these centers is more conducive to technological and intellectual innovations. These three factors alone (there are many more) give tremendous advantage to the farmers over the hunter gatherers. An individual hunter gatherer might win a fight with an individual farmer, but a group of well-fed farmers with more sophisticated weapons would have a tremendous advantage over a less populous group of hunter gatherers. Indeed, it has almost always been the case that hunter gatherers are either killed by the farmers or assimilated into the farmer's civilization.[4]

While many have attributed the cultural advantage of farmers to their innate intellectual, religious, technological or racial superiority over hunter gatherers, Diamond cogently argues that cultural advantages are based on geography and environment. His argument cannot be recreated here; however, two examples are illustrative. First, of the eight foundation crops of the Fertile Crescent (wheat, einkorn wheat, barley, pea, chick pea, lentils, bitter vetch and flax) only flax and barley existed in nature outside the Fertile Crescent.[5] To be sure, eventually all crops indigenous to the Fertile Crescent were planted in other regions, but they did not *originate* in these regions. Thus, it was the abundance of plants capable of being domesticated, rather than innate characteristics like superior intellect or race, that gave the people of the Fertile Crescent their cultural advantage. Like all human beings, the people inhabiting the Fertile Crescent were extremely familiar with the qualities of nearly every local plant. They simply had more plants to consider, and fortunately more indigenous plants were capable of domestication in their region.

The domestication of large animals also proves advantageous to a culture. Large domesticated animals provided power to till the lands, fertilizer for the lands, a protein source for the people, and, as strange as it seems, diseases. Many diseases like smallpox and measles are of animal origin. Over time, the people in contact with these animals became less susceptible to these diseases. They could, however, be carriers capable of infecting people of other cultures. The military advantages are obvious.[6] Like the domestication of plants for farming, the domestication of large animals also depended on the environment. Eurasia had 72 species of large animals as candidates for domestication. Thirteen such species were domesticated. The Americas had 24 species, and only one species was domesticated. Australia had only one candidate which was not domesticated. Sub-Saharan Africa could not domesticate any of its 51 candidates.[7] One might question why some cultures were able to domesticate large animals and others were not. According to Diamond, this has more to do with the animal than anything else. He argues that domestication is analogous to a marriage. In a marriage, the couple must reach accord on a variety of things like money, sex, religious or moral values, raising children, dealing with in-laws, etc. If just one of these issues is problematic, the marriage may not last. So it is with the domestication of animals. Many things must go right for an animal to be domesticated. If one thing is wrong, the animal cannot be domesticated No amount of human ingenuity can domesticate a hippo, zebra, lion, or gorilla because of the innate nature of these animals.[8]

Diamond describes many other non-human factors that have contributed to the current state of inequality between peoples and cultures, and his book brilliantly discloses how these factors continue to contribute to these inequalities. The argument that follows in this present book suggests that morality – our knowledge of good and evil – blinds us to the origin of these inequalities. It does so by establishing arbitrary standards that draw the moral divide between good and evil. Morality justifies the victors and marginalizes the vanquished. Furthermore, it reckons that the inequalities that exist between the victor and the vanquished are based on the victor's innate superiority. Morality ranks the victors over the vanquished. It justifies these rankings making them appear natural or of divine origin.

Morality justifies ranking, hierarchy and oppression. First, it establishes the moral divide between those deemed good and those deemed evil. It then ranks entities according to an arbitrary understanding of good and evil. The best are ranked highest. The worst are ranked lowest. The merely good are placed below the better ones and above the bad ones. This may sound simplistic, but all great civilizations are arranged in this way. They may have differing moral criteria that determine rank, but the hierarchical structure is the same. It existed in Egypt, Babylonia, Persia, Rome, China, Japan, the medieval Church, the Incas, Mayans and Aztec civilizations of the Americas, Nazi Germany, England, the Soviet Union and the United Sates.

Morality is the way civilizations great and small sleepwalk through life. It provides a way to "think" about inequalities that neither stresses the mind nor implicates the privileged ones. Morality states that the privileged ones deserve their rank because our arbitrary knowledge of good and evil demonstrates that the privileged ones are better than others. This more or less justifies anything they happen to do before they do it! The Protestant work ethic is illustrative of this moral pattern. The early American Protestant world was largely Calvinistic. Calvin thought that before time began God chose to save some and damn the rest. This meant that there was nothing a person could do in this life to be saved if that person were not part of God's elect in the first place. Within Protestant circles, therefore, the question, "How do I know that I am of the elect?" became an important question. There were many answers that were far more "spiritual," but the Protestant work ethic became one important way to determine one's election. The work ethic stated that God would bless the labors of His elect. If a man became rich, this was evidence of the fact that God saved the man. This is obviously a convenient moral system for those who happen to be rich!! Indeed, it justifies the rich ones without, at the same time demanding much from them other than they remain rich! It also accounts for inequalities in wealth and power in an interesting way. It says that inequalities are the consequence of a decision God made about salvation before time began. Thus, the rich are absolved of any responsibility for the poor. God's primordial decision is the reason for inequalities. Who can fight that?

The Protestant work ethic is a good example of how moral systems function to justify the privileged ones and absolve them of their responsibility for the needy. It is an excellent example of how morality functions within civilization. It shows how morality can answer all the questions concerning social inequality in a way that favors the status quo even before these questions can be raised. Fortunately, there are other ways to live and order life that give hope for all life forms and not just the powerful few. The first chapter will begin our discussion of such alternatives by distinguishing between the dominator model and partnership ways. It will show that human beings have, on many occasions, lived relatively free of hierarchy, ranking, and domination that moralities like the Protestant work ethic support. The Iroquois Confederacy will be discussed, but many more cultures have existed, exist, and are emerging that lack or are eliminating the hierarchical characteristics of civilization.[9] The dominator model is only one sort of culture. Today, it is culture's dominant form. This is unfortunate because this way of ordering life may no longer be able to support and sustain life. A new way of arranging the social order is necessary. Ethics, rather than morality, is one such way.

The second chapter discusses the most important reason to abandon morality in favor of ethics. Morality is death-dealing. For example, one of the most fundamental myths by which we live asserts we are all engaged in the cosmological struggle between the forces of good and evil. This cosmological struggle is played out in the battles between the Red Sox and Yankees. We see it enacted in the struggle between the Democrats and the Republicans. Our motion pictures display the triumph of good over evil in a saga like *Star Wars.* The death-dealing consequences of this belief can be glimpsed if we realize that those who flew the planes into the Pentagon and the World Trade Center on September 11, 2001, believed they were engaged in this cosmological struggle between the forces of good and the forces of evil. Moreover, those who responded with violence to this tragic event also thought they were engaged in this struggle. The false but widespread belief that we are engaged in a cosmological struggle between good and evil justifies the carnage created by the war and violence that forever plagues civilizations.

Chapter 3 shows how morality shapes civilization's thought, discourse and its social order. Its arbitrary standards of good and evil justify social hierarchies. Using moral standards that modern governments call policy, people are categorized and ranked. Some are designated more or less worthy. Others are deemed more or less unworthy. Our moral codes make these determinations. Chapter 4 argues that Nazi Germany was particularly effective in making these moral determinations. Not only will the logic of the Holocaust be discussed in Chapter 4, but it will be argued that Nazi Germany was not the moral malfunction we often take it to be. Instead, Nazi Germany was a product of civilization's need to rank. While Nazi Germany was not inevitable, it is consistent with the inner logic of both morality and the civilization morality serves.

Morality's universal function is to justify those deemed good and marginalize (even kill) those deemed unworthy or immoral. This universal function operated in Nazi Germany's efforts to kill the Jews and other "undesirable" people, but it also operates in everyday life. For example, conversations about the homeless or others in need usually become discussions about morality. In determining whether or not someone should be helped, people try to determine the reason for a person's need. Moral people are likely to help a needy person if they cannot find a shortcoming in his or her character contributing to the need. Support is unlikely if a moral flaw is detected. Moral people want to know if the person in need belongs on the "good" side of the moral divide. Help is likely to be offered if the person in need lives in accord with good moral standards. Help is not so likely if the person in need has a moral flaw. In helping us sort out the good ones from the bad ones, our moral principles also justify us when we choose not to help a needy person. In other words, our morality justifies us when we leave a person in need for dead. Most people firmly believe that hope for civilization is rooted in morality. They believe that all would be well with the world if people followed a universal moral code. Chapters 2-4 argue quite differently.

The attack on morality that occurs in the early chapters of this book might lead a person to lose hope for the wellbeing of human life on this planet. This is not so. Another way of living is proposed in chapters 5 and 6. This way is called ethics. Because ethics is reasoned behavior in the service of life, it differs from morality. For one thing, ethics resists morality's most fundamental act – drawing the moral divide between the "good" ones and the "evil" ones. Whenever morality marginalizes the unworthy or immoral, ethics identifies with those morality has left for dead and seeks to support their lives. This is a difficult but not impossible task. It is difficult because identification with the marginalized requires acknowledging that the moral standard of one's own civilization is not sacred.[10] The ethical task also requires a critical sense that can be learned through the study of people who have managed to achieve such a critical sense in the past. (Jesus and other prophets of Israel, Socrates and Siddhartha are among those worthy of such study, but they are not the only ones). Furthermore, the ethical one must have the social acumen to recognize who is marginalized. This is a difficult task because the ones morality leaves for dead are often so close to death that they do not make a sound. They must be discovered. They must be found, and when they are found, the ethical one must be skilled in the art of listening. Listening is the ability to make an adjustment in one's life on the basis of what one has heard. It is only by making such adjustments that the needs of others can be met. Help offered without listening is never actually help.

Morality serves civilization. Ethics serves life. They are different because they serve different masters. The most fundamental characteristic of morality is the distinction it makes between the good and the evil. This leads to certain tactics like hierarchy building and the rational justification of hierarchy and ranking. Moral thinking proceeds to marginalize and perhaps kill those it designates as evil. Since ethics serves life, it always identifies with those marginalized by morality. Ethics also has certain tactics. Whereas morality communicates from an unmoved center to the periphery, listening –making an adjustment in one's life on the basis of what was heard - is an ethical tactic. Whereas the end of moral reflection is justification, confession is the beginning of all ethical inquiry. Whereas mastery is an important virtue for those at the pinnacle of the hierarchies created by morality, humility is an ethical virtue. Chapter 6 discusses these ethical tactics in more detail. For now, however, it is important to know *that a partnership way is actualized simply by implementing or performing any ethical tactic or virtue, and the partnership way will last as long as such tactics are employed.*

While Chapter 6 will discuss this contention in some detail, the ethical virtue of humility is one simple example of the plausibility of this prospect. Could you imagine what a different world it would be if the foreign policy of the United States or any world power employed a little humility rather than arrogance? Wars might have been avoided. We might live in a different world. The Treaty of Versailles reveals this possibility. Conventional wisdom tells us that if the victorious allies had conducted themselves with a little more humility in "negotiating" the end to World War I, World War II might have been avoided. If World War II had been avoided, we might not have invented nuclear weapons. We would now be living in a different, safer world. The dominator system will tell us that the use of the ethical virtue of humility in foreign policy is "unrealistic," but, if our speculation about the Treaty of Versailles is correct, humility is actually life-giving.

The distinction we make between ethics and morality is unusual, but it is not new or original. Darrell Fasching has noted that word ethics is derived from the Greek word *ethos, ethike*. The word morality is derived from the Latin word *mos, mores.* Initially both words referred to the social or sacred customs of the people. In the hands of Socrates, however, ethics became the act of questioning the very sacred customs that constitute morality. Socrates refused to uncritically accept the common morality of his day. In the name of ethics he went about asking people if what they thought was good was in fact good. His questioning of morality in the name of ethics led to his death.[11]

Socrates' example leads to two conclusions. First, distinguishing between ethics and morality is not a safe, academic enterprise. Those who call the established morality into question may risk their lives in doing so. Second, engagement in ethics is not limited to Jews and Christians. It emerges anywhere the "goodness" or "sacredness" of the dominant social order is questioned.[12] In questioning the goodness of Athenian culture, Socrates engaged in ethics. The prophets of Israel were also ethical because they challenged the sacred order that the Kings of Israel and Judah tried to establish. The Buddha questioned the caste systems of Hindu society. Anarchists like Emma Goldman challenged the notion that political power and government should determine what was right and wrong. Mahatma Gandhi and Martin Luther King Jr. challenged the "goodness" of their respective cultures.

Ethical people come from anywhere. They are not confined to one religion, one geographical region or one political philosophy. They are often atheists. This book, however, largely focuses on Jesus and his followers because this is the story the author knows best. Jesus is not the first or the last word on this subject. Indeed, some American Indians, Socrates, the Jewish prophets and Siddhartha (the Buddha) predate him on the subject. Jesus is, however, an important example because Christianity has made him into someone who supposedly supports civilization's morality and status quo. Little could be farther from the truth. There is a huge gap between Jesus and some who claim to be his followers. I hope this gap will be exposed in this undertaking

Not all ethical people resist the dominator system. Some established their cultures before experiencing civilization and the dominator system. This group is not limited to the prehistoric. Many American Indian tribes built cultures long before experiencing civilization and the dominator system. These cultures are living but endangered examples of the fact that culture is possible without civilization (something the dominator system thinks impossible). According to Riane Eisler, these "uncivilized" cultures lived in accord with partnership ways. While the first chapter describes partnership ways in greater detail, it is important to know that these examples of partnership organize culture in accord with nature. Intuitively or consciously, these social organizations mimicked the symbiotic character of nature in their communal lives. In contrast, nature is always an adversary of the civilized ones.

It should be obvious by now that civilization is not necessarily a positive word in this book. It is always associated with ranking, hierarchy, morality, domination and unnecessary death. Just as ethics must be distinguished from morality, so must culture be distinguished from civilization. Civilization is a particular sort of culture. Not all cultures are civilized; however, civilized cultures always mistakenly believe that their purpose is to civilize uncivilized cultures. The perpetuation of human life, however, may depend on the civilized ones abandoning this practice.

Most civilized human beings have great difficulty understanding that culture is possible without civilization, and, as a consequence, the civilized ones usually think that being uncivilized is something to be overcome. When our civilized predecessors encountered different cultures, they uncritically described the people they encountered as savage, heathen, primitive or uncivilized. Today we call them "underdeveloped." These arbitrary definitions or significations help justify our efforts to kill the uncivilized savages, convert the heathen, rob indigenous populations of their wealth, assimilate the uncivilized, or develop the underdeveloped.[13] Our tunnel vision has prevented us from noticing many examples of sophisticated but uncivilized cultures. The Iroquois Confederacy of five North American Indian tribes is one such example. It had a written constitution that predated the European presence in the Western hemisphere. Indeed, some of the more profound, non-hierarchical elements of the constitution of the United States may have been derived from the Iroquois constitution.

The second source from which ethical people have emerged is people who resist the death-dealing aspects of morality and civilization from within civilization itself. The Biblical nation of Israel, for example, begins with Israel's God opposing Egypt – the archetype of civilization. Israel is ethical whenever it is faithful to this origin. In accord with Judaism's prophetic heritage, Jesus also opposed the death-dealing tactics of morality and civilization. Make no mistake, Jesus' crucifixion was not an error of moral judgment as Christians often maintain. His crucifixion was a consequence of Jesus' opposition to Roman civilization and the morality developed by the religious establishment of ancient Palestine. In Jesus' spirit, his followers tried to develop communities that were alternatives to Roman social organizations. In this way, they too were ethical rather than moral. The undeniable fact that Christianity itself embraced Western civilization and became one of its chief standard-bearers should not detract from the fact that many communities of Jesus' followers opposed civilized arrangements of the social order like ranking and hierarchy.

This effort to develop an ethics without morality is very critical of civilization. As the critique becomes more scathing, it is important to remember a scene from Monty Python's comic satire on the life of Jesus called *The Life of Brian*. In one scene, politically radical Jews speak in opposition to Roman rule. With great rhetorical flare, the leader asked, "What has Rome ever done for us?!?" He thought he was asking a rhetorical question, but someone in the audience responded, "Well – there are the roads." The audience murmured in agreement. The leader then said, "OK. With the exception of the roads, what has Rome ever done for us?" The audience now really got into the question. Conversation ensued whereby it was determined that in addition to the roads, Rome had provided education, better sanitation, the aqueducts, a better economy, jobs, entertainment, trade and had lowered crime. The speaker responded, "OK, with the exception of education, roads, better sanitation, the aqueducts, a better economy, jobs, entertainment and safety, what has Rome done for us!!"

This presentation risks being perceived just as outlandishly. Civilization has, in fact, accomplished many great things, but, like Roman civilization, many of the remarkable things civilizations have done were accomplished at the expense of life. America was built on the backs of African slaves, white indentured servants, impoverished workers, Chinese and European immigrant laborers and the forced eviction of the native population who we nearly extinguished in our efforts to farm the place. Chapters 2 and 3 argue that such violence is quite understandable (not justifiable but understandable) and consistent with the principles of civilization and morality. The issue is, can we keep the accomplishments of civilization and eliminate its death-dealing tactics? Ethics is a way to do just this. It is difficult because it demands a sort of critical consciousness that is only recently emerging. Morality actually prevents the emergence of the critical consciousness required to transcend civilization and create a new way of life because it provides a path of least resistance for the intellect. The critique of morality that takes place in the first four chapters may upset those who think that morality is part of the solution. It is not. Ethics is part of the solution; however, one must grasp the dimensions of the difficulties morality imposes before discussing how ethics might be a remedy.

Chapter 1:

The Dominator System and Partnership Ways

> "It is certainly true that he who holds the power to
> define is our master, but it is also true that (she)
> who holds in mind an alternative definition can
> never quite be his slave."

Neil Postman[1]

When we are born, we are thrown into the midst of political and religious madness. We never asked for this. It was not our plan. Most do not even notice. As fish do not know they are in water, we cannot recognize the conditions in which we live. We think it is reasonable to return violence for violence. We prepare for war and call it preparation for peace. We kill in the name of a loving God. We value national security far more than love or freedom, and we always confuse justice with revenge. We call this normal.

This "normalcy" extends to our work, our communities and even our most intimate relationships. Brothers and sisters are at war with one another. Neighbors hardly know each other. Forgiveness is seldom practiced. We insist on our own personal rights and degrade the needs of others. We pass this way of life from generation to generation. We perpetuate it through our actions and words. Each day we live with the consequences.

Our situation is not unique. From the dawn of civilization, human beings have been thrown into the midst of such madness. Roman gladiators entertained the masses with violence and death. Aztec priests offered human sacrifice to placate their gods. Pharaohs killed many of the slaves who built their elaborate coffins. Spartans exposed their "inferior" babies to the elements. Medieval priests, bishops and Popes led the slaughter of heretics and Jews. Civilized Europeans killed almost all the "New World's" indigenous people. Civilized and educated Germans slaughtered millions of Jews and others their government deemed inferior. The madness we call normal is not a new or isolated phenomenon.

This book discusses one important reason for our death-dealing activities and suggests alternative ways to live. The work of Riane Eisler guides our speculation. Her book, *The Chalice and the Blade*, uses archeological evidence to support her contention that around 1300 BC a great struggle ended in the Mediterranean region.[2] This struggle was not primarily a violent struggle though it certainly involved violence. It was primarily a struggle for the human mind. It was a struggle between two ways of thinking and social organization that Eisler calls the dominator model and the partnership model.[3] It is her contention that human beings lived in accord with partnership ways for thousands of years. The dominator system emerged eight to ten thousand years ago at the dawn of civilization itself and gradually won control. It is the contention of this book (not Eisler's contention) that the dominator system is a direct consequence of civilization itself.

The Dominator System

We are very familiar with the dominator system because we now live by its dictates. We have trouble even envisioning an alternative. Its logic appears synonymous with reason itself. *Ranking is the dominator system's (and civilization's) most fundamental characteristic.*[4] The dominator system does not exist without ranking. Ranking, instead of physical location, informs us of our proper "place" in the world. We must rank everything. Men are ranked above women. White people are ranked above people of color. People of color are sometimes ranked according to their complexion. Adults are ranked above children. The rich are ranked above the poor. Clergy are ranked over lay people. Employers are ranked above employees, and certain jobs are superior in rank to other jobs. Nothing escapes our compulsion to rank. Abraham Maslow has created a Hierarchy of Human Needs. IQ tests rank intelligence. *U. S. News and World Report* annually publishes the "exclusive ranking of over 1400 colleges and universities." We have contests that rank chili, lawns and Christmas decorations. Ranking is the way we determine value and worth. Civilized people find ranking impossible to avoid.[5]

The dominator paradigm influences how we think, and, in accord with our need to rank, we think hierarchically. We distinguish between the good ones and the evil ones. We rank the evil ones below the good ones. We call the thoughts and actions of the good ones reasonable. We call the thoughts and actions of the evil ones irrational or foolish. During the Cold War, for example, the dominator model informed us that those who pursued policies of mutual destruction were sober, rational thinkers. It labeled people who spoke of disarmament "utopian dreamers." During the civil rights movement of the 1950s and 1960s, African Americans who did not push for rapid social change were deemed reasonable. Those who wanted an immediate end to America's version of apartheid were called "radical" or "emotional" or "irrational." The dominator system provides language that promotes the view that ideas, attitudes and policies that support ranking are reasonable and sound. Since the way we speak greatly influences how we think, this monopoly on language makes it very difficult to envision social alternatives to the way we now painfully live.

Riane Eisler suggests an alternative to the dominator system that she calls the partnership model. This model will normally be called partnership ways in what follows because this nomenclature better describes Eisler's own contention that there are many ways to be in partnership. One difference between partnership ways and the dominator system centers on how each paradigm treats difference and diversity. The dominator system uses difference and diversity as an opportunity to rank. Partnership ways recognize that diversity supports and enriches life.

Partnership ways do not believe hierarchy is essential to life or social arrangements. They tend to understand life organically or ecologically. Many American Indians understood and lived life in this way as the following words from Chief Seattle illustrate.

> This we know.
>
> All things are connected
>
> Like the blood
>
> Which unites one family.
>
> Whatever befalls the earth
>
> Befalls the sons and daughters of the earth.
>
> Man did not weave the web of life;
>
> He is merely a strand in it.
>
> Whatever he does to the web,
>
> He does to himself.[6]

American Indian scholar Vine Deloria Jr. articulated similar partnership characteristics with the following description of American Indian spirituality, "to exist in the world means that living is more than tolerance of other life forms – it is recognition that in differences there is strength of creation and that this strength is a deliberate desire of the creator."[7]

Partnership ways are on the decline. They have been threatened by the dominator system for thousands of years. They are not, however, mere utopian dreams or intellectual inventions. There is clear archeological evidence of partnership ways, and the memories and current practices of many American Indians demonstrate the existence of partnership ways from the beginning of the human enterprise to the present moment.

Partnership in Nature

> . . . we can rescue for ourselves some of our old evolutionary grandeur when we recognize our species not as lords but as partners; we are in mute, incontrovertible partnership with the photo-synthetic organisms that feed, the gas producers

that provide oxygen, and the heterotrophic bacteria and fungi that remove and concert our waste. No political will or technological advance can dissolve that partnership.[8]

Human beings lived according to partnership ways because partnership ways mimic nature. This assertion demands discussion because conventional scientific wisdom has convinced us that competition and conflict are nature's most essential features. The fittest individuals survive and pass their genes on to the next generation. The weak do not get the opportunity to reproduce. The mere fact that something is alive indicates success in a life and death struggle that the poet Tennyson has described as being "red in tooth and claw."

In recent years many biologists have been quite critical of this conventional wisdom. While they admit that there is struggle and competition in nature, they are also convinced that cooperation and partnership is more responsible for life's persistence and evolutionary change than is competition. Professor Lynn Margulis is at the forefront of such thinking.[9] Her difficulty with the conventional wisdom of her discipline (a conventional wisdom she has done much to change) stems from scientific observations; they are not a product of ideological assertions.

She objects to the belief that competition is the most fundamental aspect of nature because this belief is derived from the animal kingdom. Clearly, struggle occurs quite openly in the animal kingdom; however, animals are not the first life form. Prokaryotes are. We normally call prokaryotes bacteria. Bacteria are living cells without nuclei. They emerged around 4 billion years ago. Bacteria are the foundation of all life in the sense that they are capable of living in the absence of other life forms while other life forms would perish without bacteria.

In Margulis' opinion, bacterial life reveals the symbiotic or cooperative character of life at the most fundamental level. Bacteria evolve in three ways. Mutation is the most familiar. Under optimal conditions, certain bacteria can divide every twenty minutes. If such reproduction were to continue for two days, the number of bacteria descended from the original would be greater than the number of all human beings who had ever lived. In the unlikely event that this reproduction would continue unabated for four days, the number of bacteria would be greater than the number of protons that physicists estimate exist in the universe.[10] This rapid reproduction is mentioned because one in a million of such divisions - a relatively frequent occurrence given the huge number of bacteria and the rapidity of bacterial reproduction - produces an offspring that is not identical with its parent. These are called mutants. Most mutants die, but successful mutants reproduce and their population expands.[11] For many years, scientists thought mutation was the only way evolution occurs, but now they know evolution occurs by other means as well. Mutation is actually the slowest way bacteria evolve.

Cooperation best describes the other ways bacteria evolve. In recent years, scientists have discovered that prokaryotes (bacteria) engage in a sort of genetic engineering. They routinely and quickly transfer different bits of genetic material from one bacterium to another without the aid of reproduction. In other words, bacteria can also evolve by recombining their DNA. At any given moment, each bacterium has the use of accessory genes from very different strains of bacteria. A bacterium can use these genes to perform functions that its own DNA cannot perform. The speed of such recombination is far superior to any adjustment that might be accomplished through mutation. As a matter of fact, bacteria can change on a world wide scale in a matter of years.[12] We encounter this ability in epidemics and in the well known ability of bacteria to resist antibiotics.

Other important microbial evidence for the fundamental status of cooperation and symbiosis in nature comes from studies of the mitochondria. Mitochondria are membrane wrapped and found inside the cells of all plants, animals and fungi. They have their own DNA that is separate and different from the DNA found in the nucleus of the cell. Mitochondria reproduce by simple division but at a different time from the rest of the cell in which they live. The vital function of the mitochondria is to allow all cells with nuclei (eukaryotes) to utilize oxygen. In other words, plant and animal life would be impossible without mitochondria.[13]

There is growing (but not unanimous) belief among biologists that bacterial ancestors of mitochondria took up residence inside cells with nuclei. They provided waste disposal and energy in return for food and shelter. It is thought that these symbiotic mergers became permanent and more complex life forms evolved.

Here, then, was an evolutionary mechanism more sudden than mutation: a symbiotic alliance that becomes permanent. By creating organisms that are not simply the sum of their symbiotic parts, - but something more like the sum of all the possible combinations of their parts – such alliances push developing beings into uncharted realms. *Symbiosis, the merging of organisms into new collectives, proves to be a major power of change on the earth.*[14]

Margulis speculates that symbiotic alliances like those that created cells with mitochondria may have been responsible for the creation of the first eukaryotes (cells with nuclei). Independent bacteria could have entered other bacteria without being destroyed. Instead, the foreign bacteria formed what we now know as the nucleus and eukaryotes evolved. Since eukaryotes are fundamental to all plant, animal and fungal life, this development has to be one of the most important evolutionary developments. If Margulis's speculations are correct, eukaryotes evolved through symbiosis or cooperation. They either prefigured or initiated partnership ways.

The symbiotic process goes on unceasingly. We organisms of the macrocosm continue to interact with and depend upon the microcosm as well as upon each other. Certain families of plants . . . cannot live in nitrogen poor soil without nitrogen fixing bacteria in their root nodules, and we cannot live without the nitrogen that comes from such plants. Neither cows nor termites can digest cellulose of grass and wood without communities of microbes in their guts. Fully ten percent of our own dry body weight consists of bacteria, some of which. . . we cannot live without.[15]

The macrocosm mimics the microcosm with respect to its symbiotic character. Cooperation, not competition, is fundamental to life.

The ecological and evolutionary importance of bacteria – the "lowest" life form – is a scathing critique of the notion of hierarchy itself. "Higher" life forms depend on the work of "lower" life forms. By the same token, "higher" life forms extend the work of "lower" life forms. In other words, there are really no higher or lower life forms. Life is symbiotic. It cooperates. Hierarchy – the only social arrangement the dominator system provides – has a limited role in nature. To be sure, hierarchy as an ideology exists *in our minds* as we, in keeping with our civilization's need to rank, classify life into higher and lower forms. Such intellectual and social constructs reflect our subservience to the dominator system more than anything else. Human beings need not live this way or even think this way. Indeed, absent the presence of the dominator system, human social organizations have not been hierarchical at all. Some pre-dominator social arrangements are well documented. We now turn to one such arrangement.

Culture without Civilization: The Iroquois Confederacy

When Europeans arrived in North America, the League of the Iroquois may have been the most important political unit north of the Aztec civilization. This alliance was founded sometime between 1000 and 1450 AD with a constitution they called *Kaianerekowa* or Great Law of Peace.[16] This constitution is extremely significant because it is written evidence of a sophisticated way of life that developed with minimal contact with the dominator system. To be sure, contact with the dominator system almost destroyed this way of life, but the mere existence of the Iroquois Confederacy demonstrates that culture is possible without civilization and the dominator system.

The Iroquois Confederation combined five nations: Mohawk, Seneca, Oneida, Cayuga and Onondaga. Their constitution reveals a sophisticated political organization that surpasses the constitutions of contemporary nations. As a matter of fact, the checks and balances within the Iroquois Constitution guided the Americans in the preparation of the Constitution of the United States.[17]

Article one of *Kaianerekowa* states that the purpose of the Iroquois Confederacy was peace.[18] The rest of the document concerns how the peace is to be preserved.

The Confederate Council is the first government body discussed in the Iroquois Constitution (*Kaianerekowa*). All business is conducted by two combined bodies of Confederate Lords.[19] "The first question shall be passed upon by the Mohawk and Seneca Lords, then it shall be discussed and passed by the Oneida and Cayuga Lords. Their decision shall then be referred to the Onondaga Lords (fire Keepers) for final judgment" (Art. 9). If the Mohawk and Seneca Lords unanimously agree, they report their decision to the Cayuga and Oneida Lords. Those Lords report their unanimous decision to the Mohawk Lords who report the standing of the case to the Onondaga Lords. The Onondaga Lords (fire keepers) render a decision in cases where the two bodies are in disagreement and confirm the decision if the bodies are in agreement (Art. 10). If, however, the Onondaga Lords render a decision at variance from that of the two bodies, the two bodies can reconsider the matter and compel the Onondaga Lords to confirm their joint decision (Art. 11).

It is interesting to note that members of the Council of Lords are appointed by the female members of the one family in each tribe who, according to tradition, has this task. (Art 17). It is also interesting to note that female members of other families appoint other functionaries as well. One family, for example, is responsible for the appointment of their tribe's war chief. Here too, only the females are involved in the selection process. Thus, if someone were to ask an Iroquois, "Who is in charge here?" the response would be, "In charge of what?" Who is in charge depends on the task. Authority does not depend on a hierarchical structure. Women and men cooperate. One sex is not considered higher or better than the other. "The lineal descent of the people of the five nations shall run in the female line. Women shall be considered the progenitors of the nation. They shall own the land and the soil" (Art. 44).

The females of the family with the right to select a Council Lord will choose a male of their family for the position. They should select with the following characteristics in mind.

> The Lords. . . shall be mentors of the people for all time. The thickness of their skin shall be seven spans – which is to say that they shall be proof against anger, offensive actions and criticism. Their hearts shall be full of peace and good will

and their minds filled with yearning for the welfare of the people of the Confederacy. With endless patience they shall carry out their duty and their firmness shall be tempered with a tenderness for their people. Neither anger nor fury shall (lodge) in their minds and all their words and actions shall be marked by calm deliberations (Art 24).

The Lordship title was never intended to have union with bloodshed (Art. 20). When the Lords of the Confederacy ate together, the constitution says they were not to use sharp utensils because they might cut one another by accident (Art. 57).

A man is given the Lordship title for life; however, if a Lord does not have a mind for the welfare of the people or if he disobeys the rules of the Great Law, he can be impeached. This is one of the first instances of impeachment in human history. The process is as follows. The men or women of the Confederacy can bring charges against the erring Lord. These charges will be brought through the War Chief. If the erring Lord does not listen to the complaint the first time, the complaint will be repeated. If no attention is given after the third complaint, a warning is given. If the erring Lord remains obstinate in the matter, it will go to the Council of War Chiefs who shall divest the erring Lord. If the Confederate Lords sanction this action, the women will select another of their sons to replace the impeached Lord.

The War Chiefs have been mentioned once again. They are not the undisputed leaders of the Iroquois Confederacy. It should be obvious by now that no one is. Each nation has a war chief. He is selected by the women from the family responsible for providing the tribe and confederacy with a war chief. The duties of the war chief include carrying messages from their Confederacy Lords and taking up arms in case of an emergency. War Chiefs have no voice in the proceedings of the Council of Lords, but they do watch the proceedings. They also receive complaints of the people and convey the warnings of the women to their Council Lord. Any message conveyed by the people to their Council Lord is conveyed through the War Chief. It is his duty to lay the cases, questions and propositions of the people before the Confederate Council. After presenting these cases, a War Chief does not participate in the discussions of the Council. He listens. He cannot speak (Art. 37). A War Chief can be deposed by his women or men relatives if he acts contrary to their instruction or against the constitution. In such a case, the women of his clan will select a new War Chief.

The Iroquois Constitution (*Kaianerekowa*) establishes individual rights and the rules of adoption. It respects religious diversity in the Confederation and describes conditions for war and for peace. Rarely, if ever, is unilateral, hierarchical power employed. Power is shared between the nations of the Confederacy. It is shared by men and women. *Kaianerekowa* describes checks and balances to all sorts of power, and it takes great care to assure that power is not lodged in one person. It is an amazing document that demonstrates that partnership prevailed in North America before the Europeans arrived. The Iroquois Confederacy was not established in opposition to the dominator system. It was established prior to the knowledge of the European version of the dominator system. It was a conscious effort to live in accord with nature as the words of the ritual to begin a meeting of the Council of Lords suggests.

> Whenever the confederate Lords shall gather for the purpose of holding a council, the Onondaga Lords shall open expressing their gratitude to their cousin Lords and greeting them, and they shall make an address and offer thanks to the earth where men dwell, to the streams of water, the pools, the springs and the lakes, to the maize and the fruits, to the medicinal herbs and trees, to the forest trees for their usefulness, to the animals that serve as food and give their pelts for clothing, to the great winds and the lesser winds, to the thunderers, to the Sun, to the mighty warrior, to the mood, to the messengers of the Creator who reveal his wishes and to the Great Creator who dwells in the heavens above, who gives all things useful to men and who is the source and the ruler of health and life (Art 7).

Partnership in the Bible

Riane Eisler's research led her to assert that the dominator system supplanted partnership ways by 1300 BC in the Mediterranean region.[20] This is a significant date because it was at this time that Moses confronted the Egyptians. In other words, the Biblical narrative begins with a confrontation between Egypt, a classic example of the dominator system, and Israel's God who favored partnership. Indeed, most of the Bible can be understood as a confrontation between these two world views.[21] The following tries to make this claim plausible.

Because most Christians have confused their faith in Jesus with faith in civilization, they wrongly interpret the Bible through the dominator paradigm. They think that the confrontation began when Moses came into Pharaoh's court demanding that the Pharaoh, "Let my people go." The Biblical narrative, however, begins when an unnamed Pharaoh thought the Hebrews had grown too numerous. He thought they were a threat to national security (Ex. 1: 8-10). The Pharaoh met with two midwives named Shiphrah and Puah. He ordered them to kill the male Hebrew babies at birth (Ex. 1: 16). Alice Laffey notes both the inequality and the irony in this order. "Shiphra and Puah could allow the female infants to live because women would never become powerful enough or important enough to threaten Egyptian security." As is usually the case with this Pharaoh, he underesti-mates his opposition. Shiphra and Puah continue to help the Hebrew women give birth.[22]

This story is a classic confrontation between the domina-tor system and partnership ways. Childbirth is the very center of partnership. Assisting with childbirth is the central metaphor for partnership because it supports the most vulnerable. Shiphrah and Puah were living *in* the dominator system. They were the Pharaoh's subjects, but they were not *of* the dominator system. They owed their allegiance to a different way of life. They lived in accord with a partnership way. They would prove to be formidable opponents of the Pharaoh.

They did not say a word in opposition, but they disobeyed Pharaoh's order. The Hebrew population continued to increase. This fact did not escape Pharaoh's attention. He called the two midwives to account. He tried to intimidate them demanding,

"Why are you doing this? Why are you letting the boys live?" The women calmly told Pharaoh a lie. They said that the Hebrew women are stronger than Egyptian women and give birth easily. Hebrew babies are born before the midwives arrive (Ex. 1: 15-19). Pharaoh believed the lie. The book of Exodus is one challenge to the dominator system after another. These challenges culminate in the emancipation of the Hebrew slaves. It should not be forgotten, however, that resistance begins in the Egyptian equivalent of a maternity ward. In accord with the values of partnership, two Egyptian women protected human life at its most vulnerable point. Furthermore, the women were not Hebrews. They were not part of God's "elect." *Adherents of partnership ways seldom have the proper religious or national credentials. They can come from anywhere.*

Hebrew resistance to the dominator system continued. The Hebrew slaves eventually fled Egypt for the Sinai. Almost immediately they established a new social arrangement that was an alternative to Egypt and the dominator system.[23] Once again non-Hebrew help was crucial. When Moses' father-in-law Jethro, a priest of Midian, visited, he saw that Moses was involving himself in nearly all aspects of the lives of each person. As only a father-in law could do, Jethro told Moses, "What you are doing is not good. You and the people with you will wear yourselves out, for the thing is too heavy for you; you are not able to perform it alone." (Ex. 18: 17, 18). Jethro suggested an administrative reform. He told Moses to select leaders or judges from among the people. Some would be responsible for 1000 people. Others would be responsible for 100, 50 and 10. These judges would address some of the easier disputes and questions. Moses would hear only the difficult cases. Few have adequately appreciated Jethro's reform. This is because we know quite well the organizational theory Jethro proposed. We call it "delegation of power." The Hebrews called it the judges system. It is a well known organizational theory that receives more lip service than actual implementation. Our familiarity with the theory, however, should not prevent us from seeing how novel and innovative this reform was. Jethro knew that Israel needed a new organizational structure because Israel was doing a new thing. They were creating an alternative to the dominator system of Egypt.

The new organizational system resisted ranking and hierarchy. Israel was a different sort of nation. It had no king or Pharaoh. When threatened, an inspired man like Gideon (Jg. 6, 7, 8) or an inspired woman like Deborah (Jg. 4, 5) would emerge and lead Israel through the crisis. The inspired one would not lay claim to the monarchy. He or she would usually go back to normal life once the crisis had passed. Despite the success of the judges system, however, Israel was very attracted to the dominator system. They grew tired of resisting the dominator system. They wanted to be like other nations. They wanted a king. The Biblical narrative says that the people asked their high priest Samuel to anoint a king.

In our age where we have almost completely sold out to nationalism and the dominator system, we do not notice that the Bible treats the monarchy quite negatively. Samuel was very reluctant to anoint a king, but God told Samuel to do so. In what might be called a last ditch effort to resist the anointing of a king, however, God told Samuel to warn Israel about the prospect of having a king.

> These will be the ways of the king who will reign over you: he will take your sons and appoint them to his chariots, and he will appoint for himself commanders of thousands and commanders of fifties and some to plow his ground and to reap his harvest and to make implements of war and the equipment of his chariots. He will take your daughters to be perfumers and cooks and bakers. He will take the best of your fields and vineyards and olive orchards and give them to his courtiers. He will take one-tenth of your grain and of your vineyards and give it to his officers and courtiers. He will take your male and female slaves and the best of your cattle and donkeys and put them to work. He will take one-tenth of your flocks and you shall be his slaves. And in that day you will cry out because of your king whom you have chosen for yourselves, but the Lord will not listen on that day. (I Sam. 8: 11-18).

The institution of the monarchy ends Israel's *official* attempt to live in accord with partnership ways and to resist the dominator system. Nevertheless, the Biblical God continues to work by *unofficial* means to promote partnership ways. God calls prophets. Few notice that prophets emerge as a separate group in Israel only after the monarchy begins. Before Israel had kings, the political leaders of Israel were often prophets themselves. After the monarchy, certain kings may have been deemed more or less faithful, but they were not prophets. This is so because the responsibility of the prophet in Israel was to challenge the worldview of the monarch, whether he or she was the monarch of Israel or Babylonia or Persia or Greece or Rome. A prophet always opposed the monarchy's interpretation of facts and events. He or she presented a vision of reality that was an alternative to the dominator system. Accordingly, prophets were a voice for partnership ways and alternative communities throughout Israel's history.

The New Testament continues efforts to form communities that are an alternative to the dominator system. Despite the obvious hierarchical structure of much of the contemporary church, the New Testament churches seem to have largely rejected ranking and hierarchy. In the Acts of the Apostles, for example, the church in Jerusalem is described as a community in which "no one claimed private ownership of possession, but everything they owned was held in common" (Acts 4: 32). The Apostle Paul had several non-hierarchical visions of the church. In some instances, he understood it organically. It is a body in which no part is of more value than any other part. Each part of the body that makes up the church is a vital organ (I Cor 12: 14-26). In his Letter to the Galatians, Paul recognizes that the social differences by which we rank do not apply in the church writing that in Christ "there is neither Jew nor Gentile. . . slave or free. . .male or female" (Gal. 3:28). In another Christian community, James admonished the people because they were treating people according to the rank given them by wealth (Js. 2: 1-4), and John attempted to build his churches on love.

The difference between the partnership communities urged in the Bible and the partnership communities of the Prehistoric world or the historic American Indians is that the Biblical communities were established as an alternative to the dominator system. In other words, the Biblical communities were conscious of the existence of the dominator system and tried to

29

resist it. The American Indians in North America may not have been conscious of the dominator system until the Europeans landed on their shores. Instead, they consciously tried to live in harmony with nature. As the account of the Iroquois Constitution indicates, they were non-hierarchical. They did not understand life in terms of rank. They were concerned with peace and the promotion of life. Since some Indian tribes never lived under the dominator system, they have a certain priority in this discussion. There is much to learn from the American Indians about alternatives to the way we now painfully live, but they have little to learn from us on such matters. Moreover, this is not a call to adopt the spiritual and religious practices of the American Indians. Our attempts to adopt their religious and spiritual practices may be simply stealing their spirituality like we stole their land.[24] It is, however, a call to listen to the words they still so graciously speak and to employ their wisdom as we try to formulate *our own versions* of partnership ways.

The Demise of Partnership Ways and the Origin of Morality

Eisler gives an enlightened description of the dominator and partnership models. However, she has considerable difficulty accounting for how the dominator model came to supplant partnership ways.

> We have nothing to go by but speculation on how these nomadic bands grew in numbers and in ferocity and over what span of time... about seven thousand years ago, we begin to find evidence ... of a pattern of disruption in old Neolithic cultures in the Near East. Archeological remains indicate clear signs of stress by this time in many territories. There is evidence of invasions, natural catastrophes and sometimes both, causing large-scale destruction and dislocation. Bit by devastating bit a period of cultural regression and stagnation sets in.[25]

Eisler's difficulty understanding how the paradigm shift from partnership ways to the dominator system occurred could be a consequence of her belief that the source of this shift is external to civilization. *Actually this paradigm shift from partnership ways to the dominator system is lodged in the principles, institutions and assumptions of civilization itself.* Uncivilized nomadic hordes were not the culprits.

Daniel Quinn offers some interesting speculations in this regard. In a series of philosophical novels, he shows how the agricultural revolution created conditions favorable to the dominator model's emergence, and accounts for its apparent victory over partnership ways.[26] We normally equate the agricultural revolution with the discovery of farming, but, according to Quinn, this is only a partial truth. Human beings planted and harvested crops long before the agricultural revolution. The activity of farming is not the problem. Planting and harvesting is often a vital, life supporting activity. The key to understanding the following discussion of the agricultural revolution is this. *The agricultural revolution was actually a shift in the way we **think** about food. It marked the first time we thought about food as a commodity. Prior to the agricultural revolution, food was no more to be bought and sold than the air we breathe. After the agricultural revolution, food was placed "under lock and key."*[27]

In our modern world a commodity is something that can be bought and sold for money, and we measure worth in terms of money. We call the monetization of our assets minus our liabilities our "net worth." We have trouble measuring worth without recourse to money. Money, however, did not exist when the agricultural revolution began. In a moneyless society, this "commoditization" of food means that food is exchanged for something of worth other than money. What is of worth in one culture might not be worth anything in another. One culture might say gold has worth. Another might think that shells have worth. One culture might think a certain expertise has worth. Another might value strength or artistry. When we say the agricultural revolution made food into a commodity, this means food was exchanged for something of worth, and food acquired a value in excess of its use value.

What made something of worth was arbitrary. Worth depended on what the culture determined it to be. The moment food became a commodity, food was exchanged for other items and services deemed of worth to those who controlled the food. Prior to the agricultural revolution, food was not exchanged in this manner. It was shared like we share the air we breathe, or it was exchanged to enrich relationships. The agricultural revolution began the commoditization of food. We began to pay for what was once available to all. The paradigm clash over commoditization is dramatically illustrated in the relatively familiar account of the Dutch and their "purchase" of Manhattan from the native population. When the story is told from the perspective of the "civilized ones," it is a story of how stupid the Indians were for selling the Europeans the island of Manhattan for $24. From the perspective of the Indians, however, it was the Europeans who were the stupid ones. The Indian's partnership paradigm recognized that the land was not something that could be possessed. The Indians thought the Dutch were spending money for something that was already available to them, yet incapable of being possessed by them.

Civilization has dramatically expanded this process of paying for what was once freely available. It now applies to fertilizer, health care, education, child rearing, care of the infirm and elderly and other services once freely given by people and nature.[28] Bottled water is a modern symbol of civilization's tendency to commoditize anything it can. Our tendency to commoditize extends to people. Modern education is often an effort to package ourselves in such a way that we will be hired for a job. We could easily call this practice self-commoditization.

In this speculation concerning the origin of the dominator system, the fact that the agricultural revolution was one of humanity's first technological revolutions cannot be stressed enough. Its importance, however, cannot be adequately expressed without recognizing that *a technology is never socially or ideologically neutral.* Normally, we think technology is neutral. Its value is thought to be a consequence of how a given technology is used. We think a technology like nuclear power can be used to destroy, or enrich life. We think it is up to us to determine if a technology is going to be used for good or bad purposes. This understanding of technology is far too simplistic. A given technology creates an entirely new social environment that demands new patterns of behavior and new ways of thinking.[29] According to Neil Postman,

Technological change is neither additive nor sub-
tractive. It is ecological. I mean ecological in the
same sense as the word is used by environmental
scientists. One significant change generates total
change. If you remove caterpillars from a given
habitat, you are not left with the same environment minus caterpillars; you have a new environment. . . . A new technology does not add or
subtract something. It changes everything. In the
year 1500, fifty years after the printing press was
invented, we did not have old Europe plus the
printing press. We had a different Europe. After
television, the United States was not just America
plus the television. Television gave a new colora-
tion to every political campaign, to every home, to
every church, to every industry.[30]

Important technological innovations create new ways of
living not intended by their creators. Those who created air
conditioning were just trying to cool the house during hot summer
months, but they also inadvertently changed the fabric of
neighborhood life. Prior to air conditioning, people spent hot
summer evenings outside on their porches. They got to know their
neighbors. After air conditioning, people spent hot summer nights
in the cool of their homes. Neighbors became unknown.
Neighborhoods were fundamentally changed.

The agricultural revolution's technological innovation
concerned the way we think about food, and like most new
techniques, this one also had unforeseen consequences.[31] Two of
the more obvious are as follows. When food became a commodity,
it was used for purposes other than eating. It could acquire goods
and services. It could control other people; hence, the desire for
food increased. More was produced. This meant that more land
was needed for farming. As time passed, civilizations expressed
this need for land more and more militantly.[32] By the time Western
Europe became aware of the existence of North and South
America, the militancy of our quest for land was quite high. It had
much to do with attempts to exterminate the native population in
the name of civilization and civilization's alleged ally, the
Christian God.[33] Much of the following discussion describes the
militant character of civilization and its morality. For the moment,

however, it is important to consider the idea that the demise of partnership ways is a product of civilization!! Uncivilized nomadic hordes had little to do with partnership's demise.

Population growth is the second consequence of the agricultural revolution's commoditization of food. It is a biological fact that the more food available to a given species, the more offspring that species will produce. More deer food means more deer. More squirrel food means more squirrels. More fox food means more foxes. We are often reluctant to apply these biological rules to ourselves, but humanity's exponential population growth over the last 8000 years proves this biological rule. Our food supply has been increasing almost continuously since the dawn of the agricultural revolution. With some important exceptions, our population has been growing exponentially as well.[34] Both population growth and the quest for land fueled civilization's expansion. They are the reason for civilization's aggressiveness.

For the purpose of this inquiry into the nature of morality, however, there is a subtle, but even more important consequence of the agricultural revolution. It is this. *The moment food became a commodity, human beings devised criteria that determined who was worthy of food and who was not. These criteria soon became moral criteria.* These criteria differed from place to place and society to society because each society had a different understanding of worth. This is why the content of morality differs from place to place even today. Unlike the content of morality, the function of morality (what morality does in any given culture) has always been the same. In every culture, morality has distinguished between the worthy and the unworthy or the good and the evil. This divide is of human origin. It is determined by the arbitrary and mostly unconscious values of those who controlled the food supply.

Social tranquility necessitated that the human origin of these criteria remain unconscious or be forgotten. If it were generally known that the divide between those deemed worthy of food and those deemed unworthy was of human design, the hungry ones might disregard these criteria. Consequently, an alliance between religious leaders and those who control the food supply emerged. This probably was not a conscious conspiracy. It probably was dictated by political, biological and logical necessities rather than by conscious human effort. Nonetheless, religious leaders served the system by convincing the population that the arbitrary criteria used to select those worthy of food were of divine origin. Morality was born when religious leaders sanctified these man-made moral criteria. The belief that morality was of divine origin justified the social order and made opposition to the social order less likely because opposing the social order was also opposing a god. The moral ones were good in the eyes of their god. Likewise, the deity declared the immoral ones evil. The union between religions and political leaders established morality. It made moral claims sacred and beyond criticism. The union between the religious and political leaders has persisted throughout civilization. Civilization exists where this union exists. It does not exist where this union does not exist. Modern, secular civilization is the only possible exception; however, it may well be that our managers, social scientists – particularly our economists – and our technicians provide the same function in our civilization as ancient priests once fulfilled in ancient civilizations.

The establishment of the moral divide enabled the emergence of more complex hierarchies. A few people were designated "extremely worthy of food." Others were deemed less worthy, but still definitely on the "good side" of the moral divide. The multitudes always have oscillated between good and evil or worthy and unworthy. In any case, *drawing the line separating those worthy of food from those deemed unworthy was a consequence of the central technology of the agricultural revolution, namely, the commoditization of food.* **Drawing the divide between those worthy of food and those unworthy was simultaneously the origin of morality, the beginning of ranking, the foundation of the dominator system and the beginning of civilization itself.** Indeed, all the characteristics of civilization – morality, hierarchy, ranking and the dominator system – are a logical consequence of the commoditization of food, which is the technology that initiated the agricultural revolution. These characteristics are far from life affirming activities. Indeed, they are death-dealing. At the beginning of the agricultural revolution, the death-dealing tactics of civilization - morality, ranking, hierarchy and domination - were minimal. Civilization was a local phenomenon, and the human population was not that large. Now the threat is more severe. While these death-dealing tactics probably will not destroy *life* on this planet (particularly life in microbial form), terrible consequences may await humanity and

35

many other life forms if we continue to walk the moral path. The last chapters of this book will show that there are alternatives to morality, and it is neither necessary nor inevitable that we remain moral. The next three chapters, however, will show why it is imperative that we leave this moral path. Hence, it is to the death-dealing character of morality that we now turn.

Chapter 2:

The Death-Dealing Character of Morality

> And the Lord God commanded the man, "You
> may freely eat of every tree of the garden; but of
> the tree of the knowledge of good and evil you
> shall not eat, for on the day that you eat of it *you
> shall die.*"
>
> Genesis 2: 16, 17.

The Garden of Eden story warns us of morality's death-dealing character. Unfortunately, Judaism, Christianity and Islam have not listened to its wise counsel. This familiar story begins with a prohibition. Adam and Eve are told that they may eat of any tree in the garden except the tree of the knowledge of good and evil. Adam and Eve disobey. They eat fruit from the tree of the knowledge of good and evil, and, from that day forward, humanity has not been able to understand anything except in terms of good and evil.[1] When we shop for food, we try to determine the "best" cut of meat. When we vote, we select "the lesser of two evils." The Garden of Eden story is an ancient attempt to account for the fact that human beings seem compelled to understand everything in terms of good and evil, better and best or bad and worse.

This compulsion is actually a consequence of the dominator system's victory over partnership ways. Like all major technologies, the agricultural revolution's new technology – the commoditization of food – was not intellectually neutral. In other words, a certain way of thinking was implicit in the commoditization of food. As we have seen, the moment food was commoditized, criteria were needed to determine who was worthy of food and who was not. The human mind followed this intellectual path. The commoditization of food made certain suggestions to the intellect. It suggested that those worthy of food should be called "good" and those unworthy of food be called "evil" or "bad." Morality – our knowledge of good and evil – was a consequence of this intellectual path. We were not compelled to think this way, but it was the easiest, most unreflective and uncritical way to think. Morality, therefore, is the intellect's "path of least resistance." As previously stated, morality is the way we sleepwalk through life. The distinction between good and evil easily led to ranking the good ones above the bad ones. Ranking led to hierarchy building. Hierarchy building became a principle feature of civilization. It assumed social, religious, intellectual, architectural (pyramids), artistic and astronomical form. Morality justified civilizations' hierarchies. This process was almost inevitable given the nature of the new technology – the commoditization of food.

The Garden of Eden story is an account of the seemingly universal penchant on the part of civilized people to evaluate everything in terms of good and evil. It also makes a unique and insightful claim. It says that our knowledge of good and evil is not a positive development! Indeed, the story explicitly states that death is a consequence of the knowledge of good and evil when it says, ". . . on the day that you eat from (the tree of the knowledge of good and evil), *you will die*" (Gen. 2: 17). This should give us pause. The civilized world believes the knowledge of good and evil is a positive thing. Some think this moral knowledge separates human beings from the rest of the animals. Nearly every religious group in the Western world tries to sell its version of good and evil, and we firmly believe this knowledge makes us better people.

The Garden of Eden story may be a voice from our part-nership past. *Its fascinating, but forgotten claim is that morality – our knowledge of good and evil – is a consequence of sin. It is not the remedy for sin that we always take it to be!!* The Garden of Eden story is even more radical about morality than this. It states that morality is death-dealing. Death, murder and killing are consequences of our knowledge of good and evil. Morality is not positive at all. It kills.

This is an unusual assertion. The rest of this chapter tries to demonstrate how morality's link to death is plausible. This will be accomplished through a study of the death-dealing ways morality functions in all civilizations. This is followed by a critique of the mistaken but popular belief that the human race participates in a cosmological struggle between good and evil.

The Death-Dealing Function of Morality

The relationship between morality and death has a subtle dimension that can be illustrated by distinguishing the content of morality from its function. The content of morality is most familiar and easiest to describe. It includes claims that certain beliefs, actions, attitudes and thoughts are good and right, and others are bad and wrong. It also includes rational justifications and arguments in favor of moral claims. The content of morality differs from culture to culture, from community to community and even from person to person. It can change over time within a particular community. The Church of Jesus Christ of Latter Day Saints (the Mormons) once claimed that polygamy was good and desirable. Today, however, orthodox Mormons reject polygamy. In other words, the Mormons changed their understanding of the content of good and evil. Likewise, the content of morality differs within a given civilization. In contemporary America, for example, many think abortion is a viable option. Others believe it is an evil on the same level as a Nazi death camp. The content of morality differs from community to community and from person to person.

The function of morality refers to what morality actually *does* within a given civilization. Unlike the changing and variable content of morality, the function of morality is always the same. It is universal.[2] *Morality always separates the good ones from the bad ones.* This process – universal to every moral code - identifies and condemns the bad ones. It justifies the good ones who, usually for moral reasons, marginalize the bad ones. Examples of how morality functions abound. In the United States, the work ethic is one of our moral beacons. It places those who work on the good side of the moral divide, and it locates those who are able to work but choose not to work on the bad side of the line. The work ethic has some sympathy for those thought unable to work and states that society should be somewhat responsible for these people. The work ethic, however, has no sympathy for people it deems capable of work but who choose not to work. If such people do not have independent means, they are marginalized and left for dead.

Nearly all Americans think the work ethic is equitable and fair. All of our political leaders think so. Liberals and conservatives will disagree on the number of people who are actually unable to work, but they agree that society is not responsible for the well-being of anyone who can work but chooses not to work. The point of this example has nothing to do with the validity of the work ethic per se. Under the dominator system, it is very difficult to understand how any society could function if people did not do some undesirable work. This example is merely an illustration of the fact that moral codes always marginalize those deemed immoral no matter what the standard of morality is. In the case of the work ethic, those who can work but choose not to work are marginalized.

Other moral codes function in the same manner. Ancient Judaism drew the moral divide between the clean and the unclean. It labeled sick people unclean and justified this action with a theology that maintained that sin was the reason for all illness. Accordingly, confession of one's sin was thought to be the first step in a person's recovery. If illness lingered, the confession was deemed inadequate. The sick person was marginalized and cut off from most social contact. The dominant theology (ideology) surrounding illness made the sick person responsible for his or her illness.

The book of Job can be read as an attack on this moral code. The very first verse of this story tells us that Job was "blameless and upright" (Job 1:1). The theology of the day stated that a blameless and upright person could not suffer; yet, Job suffers. Moreover, the cause of Job's suffering is no mystery to the reader. The story tells us that Job suffered because of a wager made between God and Satan (Job 1: 6-12). This bet does not make God look very good, but it is a factual part of the story.

The book of Job should be read as a bad visit from Job's concerned friends. It records three speeches by three of Job's friends as well as Job's response to each speech. All of Job's friends maintain the conventional wisdom of the day. They try to get Job to acknowledge and confess his sins so that the process of healing can begin. After each speech, Job maintains that he is blameless and innocent (which the story maintains is true). His friends *know* that this cannot be true because their moral ideology informed them that suffering is always a consequence of sin. (In other words, Job's friends knew the remedy before any empirical knowledge of the disease). Their patience with Job grows short. Finally, each of Job's friends has no alternative but to abandon Job. Adherence to their moral code left them no other alternative. It prevented them from ministering to Job in his pain and suffering. Their morality had functioned as all morality does. It allowed the "good" people to marginalize the "evil" one. It also justified Job's "good" friends when they eventually left Job for dead.

The book of Job is an outstanding Biblical example of the function of morality. Morality always justifies those on the good side of the moral divide and marginalizes those it deems evil. In the 9th chapter of the Gospel of John, Jesus' disciples express a slightly more liberal version of this moral code when they ask Jesus, "Rabbi, who sinned, this man or his parents that he was born blind" (Jn 9:2). Jesus' response rejects the moral code implicit in his disciple's question and thereby rejects the marginalizing function of morality itself. "Neither this man nor his parents sinned; he was born blind so that God's works might be revealed in him" (Jn 9: 3). Jesus is not saying that suffering is never a consequence of a person's sin or stupid actions. He is simply saying that suffering has many more causes than one's sin, stupidity or mistakes. In this isolated case, the reason for the blind man's suffering was so that the work of God might be revealed in him. In other cases the reason or cause of suffering might be different. The point is that it is impossible to know why someone is suffering *a priori*. (A related point is that a moral person will

41

often think he or she knows the reason for suffering before considering any evidence). It is, in fact, impossible to know the reason someone suffers by virtue of one's theology. The reason must be determined on a case by case basis. Unlike Job's friends, Jesus could minister to the suffering man because Jesus was unencumbered by morality and its need to marginalize. Jesus paid no attention to the moral codes of the dominator system in this episode. Moreover, this episode is not unique. Jesus routinely refused to judge people in terms of his civilization's moral divide. Accordingly, he always ministered to people the dominator system had marginalized as unclean sinners.

Establishing the moral divide between good and evil is the first and most devastating step in the moral process. This most important moral function *always* marginalizes someone. It *always* leaves someone for dead. It *always* classifies someone as unclean, evil, unworthy, immoral or unfit. To be sure, the marginalized ones are marginalized for different reasons in different civilizations because the content of morality differs from civilization to civilization. Nonetheless, morality's function remains forever the same. It *always* draws the line between the good ones and the evil ones, and it *always* leaves the evil ones for dead.

Nazi Germany drew their moral divide between the Aryan and the Jew. They deemed the Jews evil. They marginalized them and eventually killed them. If this discussion of the death-dealing consequences of the function of morality is accurate, Nazi Germany was not the moral malfunction we often take it to be. Nazi Germany's problem was not that it was uncivilized. Nazi Germany was in fact very consistent with the tenants of morality and civilization.[3] The Holocaust would have been impossible without an educated work force, a sophisticated bureaucracy, a high level of technology and an intellectual and religious heritage that supported or at least ignored Nazi activities. To be sure, Nazi Germany was not a necessary consequence of morality. The Holocaust did not have to happen; however, Nazi principles are quite consistent with the principles of civilization and morality discussed here. Like all civilizations in the grip of the dominator system, the Nazis established the moral divide. They separated those they deemed good from those they deemed evil. They labeled the Jews and Gypsies inferior and sub-human. Eventually, this moral scheme enabled the highly sophisticated Nazi bureaucracy to execute these marginalized human beings. Nazi attempts at genocide may have been extremely efficient, but they were not unusual within civilization.

Years before the Holocaust, the Puritans made similar demarcations between themselves and the long-time residents of the New England lands they coveted.

> The Indians were not willing to forsake their cultures for "civilization." Nor was English technology an attraction; in many instances Indian technology and know-how rivaled or were superior to the technology and know-how of the English. The Indians were willing, however, to share, and in several instances, for longer or shorter periods, this sharing took place, but the cultural language for this notion of sharing with the Indian never came into being. The Indian was, in all the reigning (European) languages, ultimately taken as a race apart and different from the European. Once the differences between the two groups came to be seen as important and continuing, it is a short step to seeing the different life of the Indian as less valuable than the European way of life and attributing the differences to qualities inherent in each group.[4]

The Puritans differed from the Nazis in this respect. Their attempts to slaughter the indigenous population were grounded in an inherited religious culture that distinguished between the elect and the lost. With such language in everyday use, it was just a short step for the Puritans and other colonists to draw the moral divide between themselves and the American Indians.[5] The Puritans believed they were on a mission from God. They came to believe that those who were different from them were not among God's elect.

This moral/religious demarcation justified almost any atrocity they committed against the Indians. These demarcations enabled the Puritans to believe they were doing God's work when they indiscriminately butchered the Pequot people in the 17th century. Two centuries later, the 1832 U.S. census disclosed the

43

efficiency of the Puritan attempt to destroy these people. The census revealed only 40 Pequot people had survived the two centuries of Euro-American domination.[6] One justification for the destruction of almost all of New England's American Indian population is the moral divide. European Christians drew this line with the words they used. They called themselves "the elect." They said the Indians were from Satan. In the oldest surviving news ballad from New England titled "Some Meditations Concerning Barbarous Natives" (1675), American Indians appear as vermin. The rhetoric is remarkably similar to Nazi rhetoric against the Jews and Gypsies. American Indians are denied human characteristics. Accordingly, it was easy to place them on the evil side of the moral divide. The Christian God is invoked to sanction this moral divide.[7]

Certainly some Puritans like John Eliot tried to "protect" the Indians who "chose" to convert to Christianity, but even conversion had a genocidal consequence. Conversion required the convert to reject his or her family, tribe and culture and adopt European ways – the ways of the dominator system. Such assimilation was a more "liberal" solution than annihilation, but it was still a form of genocide in the sense that assimilation meant the destruction of Indian culture without the necessity of killing the individual convert.[8] Assimilation rejects the notion that the culture of the other human being could possibly have anything to offer or anything from which to learn.[9] The tragedy of America is that we preferred to kill American Indians rather than listen, and we justified our atrocities with doctrines developed by Western philosophy and Christianity.

The Cosmological Struggle between Good and Evil

The cosmological struggle between good and evil is one important myth by which we live. It is further evidence of the death-dealing aspects of morality because this struggle between good and evil is either the cause of or the justification for much of the world's carnage. Those who flew the planes into the World Trade Center and the Pentagon firmly believed they were acting on the side of good against the evil Americans. They were willing to die and kill thousands to strike a blow for good against evil. We who fight terrorism believe with equal fervor that we act on the side of good in the struggle against evil. Countless lives have been sacrificed on altars of this alleged conflict between the forces of good and evil.

It has been mentioned that Christian theology normally supports the death-dealing belief in the cosmological struggle between good and evil. We have noted that the entertaining and seemingly innocuous children's book, *The Lion, The Witch and The Wardrobe* has initiated three generations of young Christians into this worldview.[10] Recently released as the Disney film *Narnia*, this "cute" story mimics Christian theology's substitution-ist atonement theories. The story reaches its climax when the Christ figure, the lion Aslan, dies in the place of the "sinner" Edmund. Like Jesus, Aslan dies to redeem the sinner. Like Jesus, Aslan rises from death. *Unlike* Jesus, however, the resurrected Aslan leads the forces of good to victory over the forces of evil. As is the case with all such conflicts, the forces of good are victorious only because the good guys are better at using the same death-dealing tactics that the evil ones employ. The objective of both sides is the same: kill the enemy.

In contrast to Aslan, Jesus never used the tactics of his adversaries. He never returned evil for evil. He prevented his disciples from violently responding to his arrest. He forgave his executioners and the disciples who abandoned him. He never led the forces of good in the slaughter of the forces of evil. Clearly, many so-called followers of Jesus think Jesus' refusal to take vengeance on his enemies is a defect in his ministry. As a consequence, they still wait for his second coming where they believe Jesus will finally correct this defect and, like Aslan, lead the forces of good in their destruction of the forces of evil. They wait in vain. They wait in vain because there is nothing in Jesus' life and death that gives one reason to believe that Jesus will come in vengeance. This misguided belief – a belief common to most Christians – is a consequence of the belief in the cosmological struggle between good and evil. Many have died serving this mistaken belief. Its source is civilization's need to understand everything in terms of good and evil.

Actually, the mere belief that one is fighting for a good cause against an evil one has death-dealing consequences that can lead to atrocious acts. Shortly after World War II, Alexander

Miller confessed the tragic dilemmas Christians, like himself, encountered in resisting the Nazis.

> . . . not to resist Nazism was to acquiesce to it. There was no living alternative to it at all. Yet to resist Nazism was to be plunged into the same chaos. For to resist one must stay alive, and one must stay alive by forgery and deceit. . . . Even within Christian groups the traitor or potential traitor must be liquidated without compunction, since not only might the lives of the group members themselves depend on it, *but the good cause itself.* . . .

> But drive this to its logical limit and where does it take us? Presumably if a man can be liquidated as a danger *to a good cause,* the same man might be tortured to make him yield information vital *to the good cause.* If he resists torture himself, would it not be more effective to torture his children before his eyes?[11]

Anything goes in the service of "the good cause." Murder is not off limits. Torture is not outlawed. Even the torture and murder of innocents is well within the realm of acceptable behavior if these atrocities serve "the good cause."

The death-dealing aspects of service to any good cause whatsoever are not limited to those who opposed the Nazi regime. In its fight against terrorism, the United States government was quite reluctant to rule out the torture of its prisoners of war. Such torture, after all, could one day serve the good cause of the elimination of terrorism or, less ultimately, prevent a terrorist act. Indeed, all parties to this conflict justify their slaughter of innocents by referring to their "good cause." Terrorists, who are in fact thought to be "good guys" by many people, justify their slaughter of innocents by the good cause they serve. We who fight terrorism are also willing to kill innocent people. We call this carnage "collateral damage." We regret such casualties of war, but we have to kill innocent people in the service of our good cause. All firmly believe they serve a good cause. Most think they are engaged in the cosmological struggle between good and evil. The tragic irony is that our dedication to our version of the good cause justifies the carnage. The death-dealing consequences of our knowledge of good and evil are revealed once more. In this regard, the ancient writers of the Garden of Eden story who revealed the association between morality and death were much more insightful than we moderns. These people were ancient. They were not stupid.

The death-dealing character of morality should now at least be plausible. The carnage associated with the misguided myth of the cosmological struggle between the forces of good and the forces of evil is one important way morality is death-dealing. Morality's universal function - drawing the divide between the good ones and the evil ones – leads to this misguided belief in the cosmological struggle between good and evil. The belief in this struggle is either the reason for or the justification of much war and bloodshed. This fact, combined with the notion that morality always marginalizes those it deems unworthy, establishes the plausibility that morality is death-dealing. The Garden of Eden story was not in error when it warned Adam and Eve not to eat of the fruit of the tree of knowledge of good and evil lest you die. They perceived something civilized ones often do not see. They understood the intimate relationship between morality and death.

Chapter 3:

Morality and the Rationalization of Racism and Oppression

> ". . . the path of least resistance is what makes the river crooked. . ."

Ani DiFranco[1]

Technology is not ideologically neutral.[2] Important technologies like the television or printing press create ways to think that can be described as the intellect's "path of least resistance." In so far as the agricultural revolution is concerned, the path of least resistance is as follows. The commoditization of food logically required the development of criteria to determine if a person was worthy of food. Priests demonstrated their value to the project by granting divine sanction to these arbitrary criteria. This established morality. The inner logic of morality demanded that we rank everything, including people, according to these moral criteria. Ranking, the definitive feature of the dominator system, was created. Ranking is "the path of least resistance" for all human intellects bewitched by the dominator system and civilization. It is not that we absolutely must rank and think hierarchically. It is just the easiest, most unreflecting and uncritical way to think.

As a consequence, Western philosophy is not the objective, disinterested quest for truth it presents itself to be. Like water always takes the path of least resistance, we think in hierarchical terms simply because this is the easiest way to think. We rank everything. We rank students, employees, sports teams, colleges and soldiers. Biological taxonomies rank living things. This has led to the ranking of people often according to skin color. Nothing escapes this need. In his book *The Working Poor,* David Shipler recognizes that we even rank our jobs according to an unwritten but well-established moral code.

> The head of a temp agency in Kansas City shivered at the notion of paying the people she placed more than $6 or $7 an hour, 'You'd fall out of whack. . . . You're off setting the entire pay scale. They're making three, four or five dollars an hour more than they should be.'

> The words 'should be' were significant. Another Kansas City employer used the same phrase to lament the rise in hourly rate from $6 to $9. . . . 'Pretty soon we've got these people who are being paid more than they really should be paid. . . .' Other employers echoed the conviction that there was a 'right' wage for a job, and that if they raised their manual laborers' pay, they would have to do the same for their foreman, accountants and executives to maintain substantial distance between salaries. . . . *It is somehow morally wrong not to pay an accountant more than a secretary.*[3]

An unspoken moral scheme justifies our hierarchical ordering of the jobs people perform. It informs us that a secretary must be paid less than an accountant and an accountant less than her boss. In her latest book, *The Real Wealth of Nations,* Riane Eisler argues that the hierarchical design of American jobs is not necessarily due to the training or education levels required for the job. Instead, she argues that the value we place on a particular job is a consequence of the low value we place on care-giving in our culture. It goes without saying that care-giving is usually thought to be the work of women. Hence, a plumber is generally paid more than a teacher or nurses' aid because our version of the dominator culture diminishes the value of women and care-giving.[4]

In any event, civilizations express their need to rank in a variety of ways. Its archeological expression, the pyramid, is found in the ruins of many civilizations. Bureaucracy is its administrative expression. The army has its generals, colonel, and majors. The Church has its Pope, Cardinals, Archbishops, Bishops, and Priests. Philosophers develop their intellectual rankings as well. Ranking and hierarchical thought are the ways the civilized ones think. As just stated, it is by no means necessary or inevitable that we think this way, but it is the easiest way to think. Unfortunately this intellectual path has had many death-dealing consequences.

Plato

Plato (c. 428-348 B.C.E.) charts this path of least resistance in *The Republic*. As is well known but rarely stated, Plato was no fan of democracy. In opposition to his Athenian contemporaries, he thought an aristocracy was the best form of government. *The Republic* is in fact an outline of this aristocratic state which resembles the totalitarian city state of Sparta instead of the Athenian polis.

Plato's state consisted of three classes: the slaves, the working class and the auxiliaries. He never actually discusses slaves in *The Republic*. They are assumed to exist, but their low status apparently makes them unworthy of philosophical discussion. This neglect is not because Athenian Greeks did not discuss slavery. As a matter of fact, some of Plato's contemporaries thought the emancipation of all slaves was consistent with Athenian principles of justice.[5] Plato, however, had little but contempt for slaves and he expresses his contempt in some of his other writings.[6]

The lower class of merchants, workers and farmers is mentioned only briefly in *The Republic*. Plato's focus is on the ruling class, which he calls the auxiliaries or the guardians. This class guards against threats to the state. When the threat is external, the auxiliary class functions as a military force. When it is internal, the auxiliaries function as police. Change is always the threat against which the auxiliaries guard.[7] Accordingly, Plato structures his ideal state to reduce the threat of change.

Plato's fear of change is a consequence of his metaphysics. He believed that the visible world in which we live is an imperfect copy of an ideal, more real, eternal realm he called the domain of forms or ideas. Whereas this visible world changes, the domain of forms is unchanging. Whereas the visible world is subject to corruption and decay, the domain of forms is incorruptible and eternal. Since the forms do not change, forms do not exist in this visible, imperfect and changeable world. At best, the things in this world are imperfect copies of the perfect, eternal and unchanging domain of forms.

Plato's moral scheme and political program can be deduced from these fundamental metaphysical principles. For Plato, the objective of any human enterprise was to make its object best resemble its ideal form; hence, it was the task of politics to make the state resemble the ideal state as closely as possible. This meant that nearly all political change should be avoided because, in Plato's view, change almost always involves movement from a more perfect condition to a less perfect condition. For the most part, Plato thought change meant degeneration. The only acceptable political change would be the sort that would reverse degeneration. For example, since Plato thought that an aristocracy was the best possible government, he would welcome a change from democracy (a more degenerate form of government in his view) to an aristocracy.

Plato believed that everything in this changeable, visible world, including the state, tends toward degeneration. As far as the state is concerned, this degenerate path moved from aristocracy, the best expression of the ideal state to timocracy, from timocracy to oligarchy, from oligarchy to democracy and from democracy to tyranny.[8] For our purposes, it is not necessary to describe these manifestations of the state in any detail. It is only important to know that any given manifestation of the state tended to degenerate into a lower, less perfect copy of the ideal state.

The Republic is Plato's effort to thwart the degeneration of the state and assure that the state remains the best possible manifestation of the ideal state. Since the greed of the auxiliary class leads to the degeneration from aristocracy to timocracy, Plato's political theory denies the auxiliary class access to private property. Furthermore, he educates his ruling class to avoid covetousness. Plato's curriculum is well documented. Of importance to this discussion is Plato always maintained a sharp distinction between the auxiliary class and the lower class. While a person from the lower class might, in rare instances, become an auxiliary, Plato believed the master class should be kept pure and undefiled by the lower class. This is why breeding and other eugenic practices like infanticide were so important to Plato.[9] In short, the hierarchy must remain intact for Plato's state to approach Plato's unchangeable ideal.

Plato thought that leaders would emerge from the auxiliary class and be identified when they approach the age of thirty. These select guardians would then be educated for the next twenty years. The best one (some might say most brainwashed) becomes the Philosopher King. The Philosopher King rules because he or she would know what is best for all people in the state. All must obey the leader. When people do not obey, auxiliaries stand ready to "persuade" them. The dictates of the Philosopher King are, after all, for the sole benefit of the state. A well ordered state, of course, benefits all its citizens.

If the twentieth century philosopher Alfred North White-head was correct when he said, "All philosophy is a series of footnotes to Plato," then Plato's vision of the good and just state shows that hierarchy and morality are part of the fabric of Western thought. Moral knowledge – the Philosopher King's knowledge of the good and evil - justified Plato's state. We find those closest to the Good perched atop Plato's political hierarchy. Those of lesser significance were accorded inferior positions. *The Republic* also reveals a curious, often unnoticed fact about the hierarchy builder himself. *Those who build and rationally justify such hierarchies have a very strong tendency to find themselves perched at or near the top.* It is no coincidence that the philosopher Plato found the Philosopher King sitting atop his hierarchical construction. In the discussion that follows, we will see that this tendency is not unique to Plato.

Plato followed the intellectual path of least resistance blazed by the social and intellectual prejudices intrinsic to the agricultural revolution. Hierarchical thinking was created by the agricultural revolution's central technology, the commoditization of food. Plato articulated the intellectual ramifications of this technology. His intellectual achievement consists in the systematic attempt to follow the intellectual path of least resistance created by one of the most powerful technological innovations ever developed. Plato's *Republic* is an astute rationalization of the social order implicit in our commoditization of food.

Hierarchy and Western Philosophy

Western philosophy's love of hierarchical thinking did not end in Plato. In subsequent centuries, it was developed, refined and incorporated into many Western systems of thought. In the early centuries after Jesus, Neo-Platonic philosophy constructed its own intellectual hierarchy. Plotinus (204-270 CE) represents the most mature form of this endeavor. His doctrine can be summarized as follows. The *One* is the source of all that exists. It is complete and perfect in itself and requires nothing other than itself. Nonetheless, entities other than the *One* exist. Plotinus' task was to account for the existence of everything else. To this end, Plotinus argued that in the fullness of its perfection the *One* overflows. The *Nous* (or rational principle) is the first consequence of this abundant overflowing. Being pure reason, the *Nous* needs something about which to think. The *One* alone exists to provide this content. Devoid of content other than the *One*, the *Nous* repeats the act of the *One*, and the world-soul emanates from the *Nous* in much the same way as the *Nous* emanated from the *One*.

Plotinus thought that the material world exists because world-soul, in multiple imitations of the *Nous*, deposits a soul (Being) in every bit of matter until matter is so saturated with Being that it cannot contain any more souls.[10] In other words, the material world has the most Being (souls) possible. This idea would later be called the *principle of plenitude*. The principle of plenitude holds that the entire cosmos is literally bursting with Being. It contains the most Being possible and is arranged hierarchically from the lowest being at the base of the pyramid of life to the *One*, alone at the summit. There is no gap in the chain of Being linking lowest being to the highest.[11] The absence of such a gap in the hierarchy of reality was later called the *principle of continuity*.

54

Obviously, this is not all that can be said about a philosopher as great as Plotinus, but enough has been said to demonstrate that, like Plato, Plotinus built an intellectual hierarchy. If Plato followed the intellectual path of least resistance dictated by the technology implicit in the agricultural revolution, so did Plotinus. In the spirit of Plato and Plotinus, hierarchical thinking became a permanent subplot in Western philosophy.

Both the principle of plentitude and the principle of continuity dominated Western thinking through the 18th century. The combination of these principles eliminated all gaps in the cosmological hierarchy. The highest realms were connected to the lowest realm by an unbroken chain of Being. Any gap in this chain violated the principles of plentitude and continuity because a gap meant the cosmos did not contain the most Being or Goodness possible. Philosophers believed such a violation undermined the perfection of the One. In later, Christianized versions of this Neo-Platonic scheme, such a gap was thought to undermine God's perfect love for creation. Theologians often reasoned that if God did not give creation the most goodness possible, God did not love creation as perfectly as He could.

By the fifth century, a Christianized version of the Neo-Platonic hierarchy emerged. The only obvious differences between the two are God rather than the *One* is perched atop the Christian hierarchy, and creation has been substituted for the Neo-Platonic eternal cosmos. Both schemes are, however, hierarchical and continue to justify the dominator system.

> Since, from the Supreme God Mind arises (and from Mind arises Soul) and since this in turn creates all subsequent things and fills them all with life, and since this single radiance illumines all and is reflected in each, as a single face might be reflected in many mirrors placed in a series, and since all things follow in continuous succession, degenerating in sequence to the very bottom of the series, the attentive observer will discover a connection of parts from the Supreme God down to the last dregs of things, mutually linked together without break.[12]

A belief in an unbroken chain (or hierarchy) extending from God to "the dregs of things" persisted throughout the middle ages. It was not without its theological critics. Most criticism centered on the contradiction between the Christian belief in an all-powerful and perfectly free God and the principle of plentitude. Some theologians thought the principle of plentitude violated God's freedom because the principle of plentitude taught that creation *must* contain the most Being and Goodness possible. Other medieval theologians thought God's goodness would be undermined if God could create a more perfect world but decided not to do so. (The thinking here, of course, reflects our bondage to morality which demands that we think of everything, including perfect worlds, in terms of our knowledge of good and evil). Nonetheless, all theologians and philosophers maintained that creation was ordered hierarchically.

The Church did not restrict hierarchy to the intellect alone. It was expressed in the Church's bureaucratic structure that ran from God the Father to Jesus to Pope to Cardinal to Archbishop to Bishop, to Priest to Laity. Nicolas of Cusa summarized this perennial philosophy at the close of the middle ages.

> All things however different are linked together. There is a genera of things such that a connection between the higher and the lower that they meet in a common point; such an order obtains among species that the highest species of one genus coincides with the lowest of the next higher genus in order that the *universe may be one, perfect and continuous.* [13]

This hierarchical understanding of creation persisted into the 17th century. Gottfried Leibniz is probably the most well known representative of the persistence of hierarchical thought. He tried to resolve the contradiction between the principles of plentitude and continuity by arguing that if God could create a better world, but chose not to do so, then God is defective. Since God has no defects, Leibniz believed God had freely chosen to create the best of all possible worlds. [14] Leibniz describes the best of all possible worlds in the following hierarchical fashion.

> Now the law of Continuity demands that when the essential determinations of one being approximate

those of another . . . all the properties of the former should also gradually approximate those of the latter. Hence it is necessary that all the orders of natural beings form but a simple chain in which different kinds like so many links clasp one another so firmly that it is impossible for the senses and imagination to fix the exact point where one begins and one ends.[15]

Leibniz was not alone in this hierarchical conception of creation. In a similar vein, John Locke expressed his version of this hierarchy. Locke, however, added an interesting wrinkle. He expressed his version of hierarchy in *biological* terms. This biological expression of hierarchy would soon become the rationale for racism and establish racism on a "rational," "scientific" footing in the minds of many.

In all the visible world we see no chasms or gaps. All quite down from us the descent is by easy steps and a continued series that in each remove differ little one from the other. There are fishes that have wings and are not strangers to the airy region; and there are some birds that are inhabitants of the water, whose blood is as cold as fishes. . . . There are animals so near of kin both to birds and beast that they are in the middle and between both. . . . There are some brutes that seem to have as much reason and knowledge as some that are called men; and the animal and vegetable kingdoms are so nearly joined, that if you will take the lowest of one and the highest of the other, there will scarce be perceived any great difference between them; and so on until we come to the lowest and the most unorganic parts of matter, we shall find everywhere that the several species are linked together, and differ but in the most insensible degrees.[16]

Hierarchy and Racism

Carl von Linne extended Locke's biological agenda in a more systematic and "scientific" form. Consistent with this agenda, Linne expanded the hierarchical order to rank human beings. In his famous work, *The System of Nature* (1735), he articulated the dominant 17th century theme that nature was created by God and ordered hierarchically. He then extended the principle of continuity throughout the human species. In accord with the hierarchical principles of the dominator model, Linne ranked the human races.[17] Other scientists and philosophers followed his agenda. As was the case with Plato, these scientists and philosophers surprisingly found themselves or their nationality or their white race perched atop their hierarchical constructions. This would be funny if the consequences were not so tragic.

Probably the most creative philosopher of the 18th century, Immanuel Kant, is both a good example of those who fabricated these racial hierarchies and a wonderful illustration of the tendency of those who build these intellectual edifices to find themselves in a privileged position on the human pyramid. Kant believed in four distinct human species, each descending from an original stem. The original stem consisted of "white brunette" people who lived between the 31st and 52nd parallels. By now it should not shock us to find that Kant believed Europeans were the best approximation of this original stem.[18] Kant then ranked the races of human beings in terms of how far each race had degenerated from the original. The top of the hierarchy belonged to blond white people found in Europe. Next in order were the copper red people of North America. This race was followed by the black race of Africa. The olive-yellow Indians were on the bottom of Kant's hierarchy.[19]

The great English philosopher David Hume might disagree with the way Kant had ordered humanity. He probably would have placed Africans on the bottom of his human hierarchy as the following infamous footnote suggests.

> I am apt to suspect the Negroes and in general all other species of men (for there are four of five different kinds) to be naturally inferior to whites. There never was a civilized nation of any other complexion than white, nor even any individual

eminent either in action or speculation. No ingenious manufacturers amongst them, no arts, no sciences. On the other hand, the most rude and barbarous of the whites, such as the ancient Germans, the present Tartars, have still something eminent about them, in their valour, form of government, of some other particular. Such a uniform and constant difference could not happen, in so many countries and ages if nature had not made an original distinction between these breeds of men. Not to mention our colonies, there are Negro slaves dispersed all over Europe, of whom none ever discovered any symptoms of ingenuity; though low people without education will start up amongst us and distinguish themselves in every profession. In Jamaica, indeed, they talk of one Negro as a man of arts and learning, but it is likely he is admired for slender accomplishments, like a parrot who speaks a few words plainly.[20]

Both David Hume and Immanuel Kant were among the greatest minds of their generations. Both belong in the pantheon of great philosophers. Yet, like Plato and many philosophers before them, they followed the intellectual path of least resistance when they uncritically accepted the validity of hierarchy. The commoditization of food created this path. They were merely following its logic. Racism is one terrible consequence.

Racist, hierarchical thinking was hardly limited to Europe. Like most American slave-holders, Thomas Jefferson defended slavery on hierarchical grounds. Even though he knew of the evils of slavery (He once wrote regarding slavery, "I tremble for my country when I reflect that God is just; that his justice cannot sleep forever."), he still tried to justify American racism.[21] He argued that slaves were by nature inferior to their masters and that slavery was a necessary evil that, for the time being, needed to remain in existence.[22]

It is interesting to note some of the arguments American slave-holders used to justify slavery. They added some interesting, almost Darwinian twists. The slave-holders of the late 18th century generally agreed with Jefferson's assertion that slavery was a necessary evil. They justified this necessary evil on the grounds that slavery prevented the violence that was sure to happen if the slaves were freed.[23] Some even argued that slavery prevented another "evil," namely, inter-racial sex. Two obvious facts were lost on the slaveholders. First, slavery did not prevent violence. Slavery is itself violent. Slavery did not prevent inter-racial copulations either. These frequently occurred between white masters and slave women. To be sure, this "sexual" activity is far more consistent with what we now call rape than it is with love, but many people were born because of these sexual relations. Slavery did not prevent Thomas Jefferson himself from fathering a large number of inter-racial descendants.

As time passed, and as the elite of the slave-holding South responded to abolitionist criticism, slaveholders began to argue that slavery was a good thing instead of a necessary evil. Thomas R. Dew of William and Mary College justified slavery by saying that since slavery is "a necessary stage in human progress," it cannot be an evil in itself.[24] Dew's theory represents an interesting adjustment to hierarchical thinking. Heretofore, hierarchy was expressed more or less statically. Under Plato's influence, hierarchy was usually conceived as an eternal pyramid. In this case, however, Dew expressed hierarchy historically. Dew's argument implies that history itself is the hierarchy, and the present is superior to the past. Moreover, in any given moment, some people are more developed and superior than others. (This understanding of history dominates a contemporary economic theory we call economic development. Here people are designated "developed" or "under-developed." These designations give people their relative value in the current world order, and allow the "developed" people to do whatever is necessary to "develop" the "under-developed" people of the world).

Other slave-holders argued in favor of slavery in more traditional ways. South Carolina's governor George McDuffy argued from the perspective of divine providence when he said that Africans were destined by God to be slaves as "evidenced by their color and intellectual inferiority."[25] In 1837, John C. Calhoun cleverly related the principles of plentitude and continuity to Dew's view of a progressive history. As Leibniz argued that this world had to be the best of all possible worlds, Calhoun maintained that slavery was the "best possible" arrangement between white Europeans and black Africans. "I hold that in the present state of civilization where races of different origin and distinguished by color and other physical differences, as well as intellectual, are brought together, the relations now existing in slaveholding states between the two is, instead of evil, a positive good."[26]

It is not that these men of the South had a moral lapse when they justified slavery. Jefferson, Dew, McDuffy and Calhoun were expressing the morality of the South. Their expressions followed an intellectual path paved by the assumptions of the technology of the agricultural revolution. Morality demanded the distinction between good and evil or the superior and inferior. These distinctions led to hierarchy both in our thought and in social structures. Hierarchical reflection led to the ranking of human beings and the ranking of human beings either created or justified racism. This outcome was not inevitable. Following the ideological path forged by the agricultural revolution might have led elsewhere. The only inevitable consequences of the agricultural revolution's technology are ranking, hierarchy and morality. How we rank, who receives supreme status and how this status is exercised is not inevitable.

Nonetheless, the reason the South does not have slaves today has nothing to do with their achievement of moral enlightenment. They lost the Civil War!! Had the South won the American Civil War, the moral system of the slaveholders would have been vindicated. The winners of wars establish the morality. When one society triumphs over another, their morality achieves dominance. Alexander the Great, for example, established Hellenistic moral standards over the region he conquered. Alexander was called "Great" because his Greek culture triumphed. Indeed, he is called "Great" today because we have not been liberated from Hellenistic morality. Others, however, understood Alexander differently. The Jews who Alexander conquered provide an alternative understanding of this man.[27]

> Alexander. . . . fought many battles, conquered many fortresses and killed the kings of the earth. He went to the ends of the earth and plundered many nations. His ambitious heart swelled with pride when the earth fell silent before him. He gathered a powerful army. He ruled over coun-

tries, nations and princes and they paid him trib-
ute. . . .

After ruling for twelve years, Alexander died. His
officers, then began to rule. . . . they put on
crowns after his death, and so did their sons and
their sons after them, *and they brought increasing
evils into the world.* (I Maccabees 1: 1-9).

This is one of only a few insights we have into how the
vanquished felt about Alexander the Great and his legacy. Today
his ruthlessness is largely overlooked. We prefer to acknowledge
his cultural legacy. He did, after all, "bless" the Western world
with the gift of Hellenism, and our intellectual heritage is
grounded in Hellenistic philosophy. By the same token, Hitler,
had he triumphed, would have made Wagner and perhaps
Beethoven much more popular.

Chapter 4:

The Holocaust: Morality in the Extreme

> "One of the least helpful ways of understanding the Holocaust is to regard the destruction process as the work of a small group of irresponsible criminals who were atypical of normal statesmen. . . . On the contrary, *we are more likely to understand the Holocaust if we regard it as the expression of some of the most profound tendencies of Western civilization in the twentieth century.*"

> Richard L. Rubenstein[1]

To most people, Nazi Germany is the antithesis of morality. They think it is the most immoral nation of all time and believe a good dose of morality would have served them well. Conventional wisdom maintains that Nazi Germany's problem was they did not know the difference between good and evil. Our discussion, however, has shown that the content of morality – what we explicitly acknowledge to be good and evil – differs from place to place. What is good in one place could be evil elsewhere. Despite the fact that moral people fervently believe their own understanding of good and evil should be universal, there has never been and there probably never will be an agreed upon moral standard. Indeed, in recent years, the closest the world has come to a universal moral standard was the middle of the twentieth century when Nazi Germany nearly achieved the power to impose its morality on the entire world. Despite the fact that there has never been a universal moral code, one thing about morality is universal and absolute. It is morality's function. Morality's universal function, not its content, is definitive of morality.[2]

Understood in terms of its universal function, morality *always* draws the line separating the good from the evil. Different moral systems disagree about where the line between good and evil is to be drawn, but morality always draws this line. *A country, person or culture is by definition moral if it draws the line that separates the good ones from the evil ones.* An outside agent might think the place a given country draws its moral divide is the wrong place to draw this line, but this does not mean the country that "misdraws" the line is not moral. It just means that two different moral standards are being used to determine good and evil.

Nazi Germany was moral because it employed morality's universal function. It drew the moral divide. It divided those the Nazis deemed good, the Aryans, from those they labeled evil, the Jews, Gypsies, Slavs, homosexuals and others they deemed inferior. This may not be where we would draw our moral divide. At the very least, we would draw it in such a way that the Nazis were on the evil side of the line. Perhaps we would even place those who fought and died opposing the Nazis on the good side of the line. One wonders, however, if the world would now take this position if the Nazis had been victorious.[3]

A nation or group or person is moral whenever it employs morality's universal function. Whenever the good people are distinguished from the evil ones, there is morality. Nazi Germany did not have a moral malfunction any more than did the slaveholders of the American South. Both adopted the pattern of morality that has been described. Both employed morality's universal function. Both drew the moral divide between the good ones and the evil ones. As the Southerners drew the moral divide between Europeans and Africans, the Nazis believed that the Aryans were good and the Jews, the Slavs and Gypsies were evil.

Nazis were aided in this belief by scientists and philosophers who "rationally demonstrated" that blond, white skinned people were superior to people with darker complexions.

Hitler, it must be remembered, was not the first to announce the racial superiority of the Aryan people. Great philosophers like Immanuel Kant and G.W.F. Hegel had already assured the German public that the German people represented the pinnacle of humanity. Moreover, the Nazis were not the first to enslave those they deemed inferior. Slavery was practiced throughout civilization. The Nazis were not the first to isolate people they deemed inferior on reservations and in concentration camps. The United States did this to its own indigenous population. The Germans, however, were more civilized than the Americans in that their more sophisticated bureaucracies and technologies enabled them to take the oppression of undesirables to new levels. This happened *because of* the high level of civilization Germany had achieved. It did not happen in spite of German civilization. It happened *because of* Germany's morality. It did not happen in spite of it.[4] Nazi Germany's crime was not that they were immoral. They were actually hyper-moral. They pushed the establishment of the moral divide to its logical, extreme conclusion! Instead of passively leaving those they deemed evil for dead (as most moral schemes do), Nazi Germany killed the "evil" ones. If the definitive function of morality is drawing the moral divide, morality was either the cause of the Nazi Holocaust or the justification for it.

Lebensraum

Time and again we have recognized the validity of Neil Postman's claim that technologies are never ideologically or socially neutral. New thoughts and social arrangements are implicit in every important technology. Morality itself is the way of thinking implicit in the agricultural revolution's chief technology, namely, the commoditization of food. Civilization and social hierarchy are social arrangements that are implicit in this same technology. We have yet to discuss population growth which is another social phenomenon implicit in the commoditization of food. Like all living populations, human population expands with the food supply. Moreover, the commoditization of food increases the food supply because it gives food more value. It can be exchanged for other goods and services. Trouble can happen, however, when moral claims are applied to expanding population. Certain moral solutions can be and have been quite death-dealing.

Thomas Robert Malthus (1766-1834) is best known for deriving his economic doctrine from this relationship between population and food supply. In his *Essay on Population,* Malthus established economics as 'the grim science" highlighting the biological claim that the number of people in the world is limited by the number that can be fed. Increases in the food supply would bring an increase in population to consume the increased food supply. This meant that the vast majority of people would always live on the verge of starvation. Malthus later adjusted these dire predictions stating that the elimination of vice (meaning sexual promiscuity) might reduce populations and allow people to live above the subsistence level. He also allowed for people to protect their standard of living by voluntarily reducing family size while the food supply increases.[5] His grim predictions have further been undermined by medical advancements in birth control, which reduce unwanted pregnancies. These and other adjustments and advancements have led some to question and dismiss Malthusian theory altogether. Perhaps this evaluation is slightly premature.

The fact is that, with some important exceptions, both the human population and its food supply have expanded since the agricultural revolution. For millennia, this was not a large problem because there was more than enough land in which to expand. More recently, excess population has become a problem. As far as Europe is concerned, much of its excess population immigrated to the Americas where Europeans displaced and destroyed much of the indigenous population. This safety valve (from Europe's perspective) was shut by American immigration laws that limited the number of immigrants. Europe had to explore other avenues to limit its population.

World War I might have been an effort in this regard. The carnage resulting from this war had no precedent. Moreover, the leaders seemed to take this in stride. About 6000 people were killed each day for 1600 days. The total number of deaths was close to 10 million.[6] This carnage was not deliberately conceived, but Richard Rubenstein has posed an interesting question:

For three centuries the peoples of Europe had exported their surplus populations to North and South America, thereby putting off the day when the inexorable fatalities to which Thomas Malthus pointed finally overtook them. In the nineteenth century, Europe also began to export its sons to participate in the newer imperialist ventures in Africa and Asia. In the twentieth century, the American frontier was closing and in spite of the continuing emigration, population continued to grow in most European countries. *Is it not possible that some automatic, self-regulating mechanism in European society was blindly yet purposefully experimenting by means of war with alternative means of population control?*[7]

Rubenstein goes on to state that the difference between the elites of World War I and the Nazi elite was that the Nazis were *conscious* of the fact that their war was to eliminate excessive population.[8]

Europe's excessive population was composed of "superfluous people" whose numbers increased in Europe between the wars. In Europe the excessive population was composed of *apatrides* or stateless people. Since a person's civil rights were determined by the state in which the person was a citizen, *apatrides* had no rights wherever they went. Like modern day refugees, they were assigned to camps where they had little choice but to remain in a sort of suspended animation. These people had committed no crime. Their status had simply been "altered" by the bureaucracy or policy.[9] The Germans altered the status of many undesirables. While the rest of Europe wondered what to do with their *apatrides*, Hitler apparently had a solution. Many people without status would eventually be killed in order to create *lebensraum* or living space for German citizens. The murder of millions was Nazi Germany's answer to overpopulation. It also may have been a way to deal with the exponential increase in population begun with the commoditization of food.

The Holocaust and German Philosophy

German philosophy justified the Holocaust, but this was not the only way the Holocaust was justified. Centuries before the German philosophers to be discussed below, Martin Luther articulated what was then and what continued to be a common Christian understanding of the Jewish people. In his treatise *On the Jews and Their Lies*, Luther slandered the Jews as he repeatedly articulated late medieval lies such as the Jews wanted to rule the world; the Jews are arch-criminals because they killed Jesus, and that the Jews are a plague and a pestilence. Obviously such rhetoric was adopted by Nazi propaganda. The sad fact is that when Hitler spoke, his racist ideology was not unlike the sermons his audience may have heard in church.

Luther's two kingdom's theory was another treatise that had a profound influence on the German understanding of the relationship between Christianity and politics. This treatise was not explicitly anti-Semitic, but it did establish a theory of government that, according to common German interpretations, allowed Christians to absolve themselves of their responsibility for government affairs. Briefly stated, Luther believed that there were two realms called the Kingdom of God and the Kingdom of Man. These kingdoms were separate and distinct. The Kingdom of God concerned what we would now call spiritual matters. The Kingdom of Man concerned political matters. Luther believed things would be fine if the Kingdom of God – as represented in the Church – would not get involved in worldly matters, and the worldly kingdom – as represented by civil government – would not get involved in spiritual matters. Today one might understand Hitler's Germany to have crossed this divide because Hitler's *Reich* clearly had many religious qualities; however, most of Hitler's Lutheran contemporaries lacked the capacity to understand it in this way. The two realms remained separate. Their separation prevented German churches from challenging Hitler.

In any case, German philosophy also justified German racism. German philosophers constructed their intellectual hierarchies. They ranked the nations of Europe as well as the races of the world. Since finding oneself atop one's own hierarchical construction is a peculiar trait of hierarchy builders, it is no surprise to discover that German philosophers found the German people perched at the apex of their hierarchy of European nations.

We have already discussed an essay by Immanuel Kant called "On the Different Races of Man" (1775). In it he argued that there are four distinct races of human beings. Each race degenerates from an original white, brunette race living in the Northern temperate regions of the planet. Following the Platonic contention that change implies degeneration, Kant asserted that Europeans had degenerated the least from the original; hence, Europeans are the superior race. Among the Europeans, Kant asserted that the people living in the Northern regions of Germany are closest to the original.[10] Immanuel Kant lived in the German town of Konigsburg in what might be called the Northern regions of Germany. It is said that he never traveled far from this town. It is said that he routinely took walks through this town and that people could set their watches according to Kant's punctuality. Kant's "discovery" that the people he encountered on these walks were the highest form of humanity should be quite humorous. Our humor has to be diminished somewhat, however, because the consequences of his "discovery" were so dangerous.

Probably of more importance than the philosophy of Immanuel Kant was the work of his younger contemporary Johann Gottfried von Herder (1744-1803). Herder is known as the forefather of the romantic nationalism that dominated 19th century Germany. Herder rejected the cosmopolitanism of the Enlightenment and held that each nation possessed a folk spirit (*Volkgeist*). This folk spirit was primarily expressed in a common language, but it also received expression in poetry and the other arts as well. While Herder did not think that one particular folk spirit was inherently superior to another, he "set the table" for the racist ideology of Nazism by noting that it was the responsibility of each nation to preserve its own folk spirit. This meant that each nation should resist foreign elements whenever possible. In other words, diversity was the enemy of the folk spirit, and the folk spirit was the essence of the nation.[11]

The philosophical basis for German national and racial superiority was even more profoundly outlined in the philosophy of G.W.F. Hegel. The mention of the name Hegel sends shivers up the spines of many students of philosophy who despair at ever understanding his thought. The real issue behind his thought, however, is not philosophical at all. It is political. Citing the concurrence of a number of Hegel's contemporaries, Karl Popper maintains that the secret to Hegel becoming the greatest 19th century German philosopher is that Hegel had the Prussian state behind him. He was the official philosopher of Prussia's absolute monarch, Frederick William.

> The best witness is Schopenhauer . . . (who) drew the following excellent picture of the master: Hegel, installed from above by the power that be, as the certified Great Philosopher, was a flat-headed, insipid, nauseating, illiterate charlatan, who reached the pinnacle of audacity in scribbling together and dishing up the craziest mystifying nonsense. This nonsense has been noisily proclaimed as immortal wisdom by mercenary followers and readily accepted as such by all fools, who thus joined into as perfect a chorus of admiration as had ever been heard before. The extensive fields of spiritual influence with which Hegel was furnished by those in power has enabled him to achieve the intellectual corruption of a whole generation.[12]

One must decide for oneself whether Hegel was a true philosopher, or just an agent of the state as his (perhaps jealous) contemporary Schopenhauer asserts. Nevertheless, it is clear that Hegel's teachings about the state are quite ethnocentric. Hegel thought any given state was a limited expression of the Universal Spirit. He thought the German state in particular was the ultimate expression of the Universal Spirit. "The Universal is to be found in the State." "The State is the Divine Idea as it exists on earth. . . We must therefore worship the State as a manifestation of the Divine." "The State is the march of God through the world." "The State is the actually existing, realized moral life."[13]

The state is the historical unfolding of the Absolute Spirit or Idea. This Absolute Spirit or Idea was not a Platonic form. It did not reside in an otherworldly domain. Hegel's Absolute Spirit expressed itself historically in the state. In fact, the state is the supreme expression of the Absolute Spirit. It follows that there is no moral authority other than the state. Absent an external moral authority, war is the way that one national moral expression demonstrates supremacy over another.

> The Nation State is Spirit in its substantive ration-
> ality and immediate actuality . . . it is therefore the
> absolute power on earth . . . . The state is the
> Spirit of the People itself. The actual State is ani-
> mated by this spirit, in all its particular affairs, its
> Wars and its Institutions . . . . The self-
> consciousness of one particular Nation is the ve-
> hicle for the development of the collective spirit; .
> . . in it, the Spirit of the Time invests its Will.
> Against this Will, the other national minds have
> no rights: that Nation dominates the World.[14]

War is the vehicle through which the absolute Spirit un-
folds. Since Hegel thought that the Prussian State represented the end of this conflict, he thought Prussia or perhaps a greater German state was the complete manifestation of the Absolute Spirit in history. It might be said Hegel believed the German state – not Jesus – was God incarnate.

Even if Hegel was not the official philosopher of Prussia, Frederick William of Prussia could not have opposed Hegel's philosophical opinions about the supremacy of the Prussian state. Hegel's influence spread. Hegel's students (of the more totalitarian ilk) were appointed to Prussian and later German Universities by the State. With modifications here and there, the ethnocentrism of Hegel's philosophy would dominate Germany for many years. It was fertile soil for Nazi ideology and Nazi morality.

The Bureaucratization of Morality in the Holocaust

Justified by this philosophical ethnocentrism, the Nazis developed their moral scheme. As is true of any moral scheme, drawing the moral divide was the first step. The Nazis did this in a very effective, visible way. They made all Jews wear a yellow Star of David. This made the moral divide readily apparent to anyone with eyes to see. It distinguished the "evil" Jews from the rest of the population. There was not a Jew who wore this badge who was not marginalized. There was not a Jew who wore the badge who was not in grave danger.

Making the moral divide visible was the first and most fundamental step in what we now ominously call the Nazi's "final solution to the Jewish problem." The Nazis quickly made other distinctions. Just as Dante ranked the residents of purgatory and hell, the Nazis ranked the Jews. German Jews were privileged over non-German Jews. German war veterans were held in higher status than ordinary German Jews. Families whose ancestors were German born were favored over naturalized citizens.[15] The Nazis formed a Jewish Council of Elders from the "most respected Jews" within a given jurisdiction. They enlisted these Councils to assist in their terrible program. Probably convinced that they were sacrificing the few to save the many, the Councils were given the number of Jews that the Nazis wanted "deported." The Council of Elders made lists of deportees. In accord with policy, "the Jews registered, filled out forms, answered pages and pages of questionnaires regarding their property so that it could be seized more easily, they then assembled at collection points and boarded the trains."[16]

The imposition of rank – the essential feature of civiliza-tion, and its dominator system – was central to the Nazis' nearly successful attempt to execute all the Jews. The imposition of the Star of David badge pacified the German public. It made it clear to those without the badge that their fate was separate from the fate of those wearing the badge. Moreover, ranking the Jews themselves created both complacency and competition between fellow Jews who may have thought that a higher status would save them from an undesirable fate.

> The Germans were notably successful in deport-ing Jews by stages, because those who remained behind would reason that it was necessary to sac-rifice the few in order to save the many. The op-eration of this psychology may be observed in the Vienna Jewish community, which concluded a deportation 'agreement' with the Gestapo, with the understanding that six categories of Jews would not be deported. Again, the Warsaw ghetto Jews argued in favor of co-operation and against resistance on the grounds that the Germans would

deport only sixty thousand Jews but not hundreds of thousands. The bisection phenomena occurred also in Salonika where the Jewish leadership cooperated with the German deportation agencies upon assurance that only 'communist' elements from the poor sections would be deported, while the 'middle class' would be left alone.[17]

Much has been spoken and still more has been left unspoken concerning the Jewish cooperation in their own destruction. It is way too complicated to condemn or justify, but some of their cooperation may be a consequence of their trust in civilization itself. Like nearly all of us, they assumed that civilization and morality serve life. This is rarely the case. The Holocaust demonstrates that civilization and morality can lead to genocide.

The great historian of the Holocaust, Raul Hilberg, articulated the moral structure of this downward spiral into genocide as:

Definition

Dismissals of Employees and Expropriation of Business Firms

Concentration

Exploited Labor and Starvation

Annihilation

Confiscation of Personal Effects[18]

The first thing to note is that this is a bureaucratic flow chart. The tasks can be efficiently performed by any modern bureaucracy should it somehow be so motivated. As is the case with any bureaucratic task, the tasks are broken down into smaller tasks. Each small task contributes to the entire process; however, each task is so small that its banality prevents the one performing the task from recognizing his or her role in the outcome. Indeed, in most cases the functionary would not need to concern himself or herself with the ultimate outcome of his or her activity. Moral concern for the outcome of any particular task would be placed with a person's immediate supervisor who also was unconcerned with the outcome.

Personal, moral considerations (in other words one's own understanding of the content of good and evil) were (and are) neutralized by the bureaucratic structure itself. Nearly all officials are taught to strive for excellent performance reviews without too much understanding of the ultimate goal of their performance. An individual's moral considerations only undermine his or her performance review.

It is important to pause here and recognize that some moral codes or beliefs are not as death-dealing as others. Indeed, danger resides in one particular moral code becoming universal as one did in Nazi Germany. As a consequence, it is in the interest of survival that competing moral schemes exist within any given expression of civilization or the dominator model. The framers of the United States constitution implicitly recognized this fact when it institutionalized the separation of powers between the judicial, legislative and executive branches of the U.S. government. In terms of this discussion, the separation of powers seeks to prevent one particular morality from gaining universal status. *As long as we operate within the dominator system* (which unfortunately is most of the time for many of us) competing moral standards prevent the tyranny of a dominant morality. This is why "value-free" bureaucracies are so dangerous. They undermine competing personal moralities in ways discussed in the paragraph immediately above as well as in other ways that will now be discussed.

Bureaucratic language, the language of expertise, is another way to distance the competent bureaucrat from the consequences of his or her actions. The following is a quotation from a report by a German technician ironically named Willy Just.[19] In case you have grown so accustomed to bureaucratic language that you do not realize what Mr. Just is talking about in this memo, he is discussing the technical difficulties he is encountering in his attempt to design a mobile gas chamber that will kill human beings.

> A shorter, fully loaded truck could operate much more quickly. A shortening of the rear compartment would not disadvantageously affect the weight balance, overloading the front axle, because 'actually a correction in the weight distribution takes place automatically through the fact that the cargo in the struggle toward the back door during the operation always is preponderantly lo-

cated there.' Because the connection pipe was quickly rusted through the 'fluids,' the gas should be introduced from above, not below. To facilitate cleaning, an eight to twelve inch hole should be made in the floor and provided with a cover opened from outside. The floor should be slightly inclined, and the cover equipped with a small sieve. Thus all 'fluids' would flow to the middle, the 'thin fluids' would exit even during the operation, and the 'thicker fluids' could be hosed out afterwards.[20]

Apparently Mr. Just's boss had given him a job to do. This was his report. Willy Just used his expertise to perfect a certain kind of vehicle that apparently was not operating as efficiently as it might. Willy's memo dealt with the flaws in the previous design. He accounted for the "cargo" that would shift to the back of the vehicle during "the operation," and he effectively addressed the near automatic expulsion of the "thin fluids." Unfortunately, he could not quite relieve those who would operate the truck of the need to hose out the "thicker fluids" that were a consequence of the "cargo's" reaction to "the operation." Willy Just's focus on the task at hand along with his use of bureaucratic language allowed Willy Just to design a mobile chamber of death without much damage to his conscience. Such moral considerations were for his supervisors alone to consider.[21]

The Holocaust was not a consequence of uncivilized barbarianism. It would not have been avoided if only the Germans were more civilized. In truth, modern civilization – with its science, advanced technology and bureaucracy – made the Holocaust possible. This is not the same as saying that the Holocaust was inevitable. It is saying that the Holocaust was a product of civilization and not the "uncivilized' anomaly it is often believed to be.[22] As Eli Wiesel tells us:

> It is possible to be born into the upper or middle class, receive a first-rate education, respect parents and neighbors, visit museums and attend literary gatherings, play a role in public life and begin one day to massacre men, women and children, without hesitation and without guilt. It is possible to fire your gun at living targets and

> nonetheless delight in the cadence of a poem, the composition of a painting. . . . One may torture the son before the father's eyes and still consider oneself a man of culture and religion.[23]

Modern bureaucratic processes seek to eliminate a bureaucrat's understanding of good and evil. *As long as people do not engage in the radical critique of civilization and morality demanded by the Holocaust and attempted in this discussion, an individual or group's moral outrage is the last line of defense against the more extreme death-dealing aspects of morality like the Holocaust.* Bureaucracy eliminates this line of defense when the individual bureaucrat relinquishes his or her moral responsibility to bureaucratic superiors. This is not only a Nazi phenomenon. The same amoral thinking was created by the bureaucracy that surrounded the invention of the atomic bomb. There was only one attempt to discuss the moral implications of the atomic bomb by the scientists working on the project, and hardly anyone thought it necessary to discuss the moral implications of what they were doing. "Indeed, when the presidential committee, appointed by Truman to decide the issue of the use of the bomb on Japan, met on May 31, 1945, the possibility of not using it was never raised."[24] At this crucial point in human history, bureaucracy proved to be impervious to moral critique.

In the past, the powerful had to fear the moral outrage of the people if they wanted to avoid revolution and keep their privileged position. The bureaucratic process, however, makes such moral outrage less likely. *The bureaucratic process itself has become the moral code.* A person is no longer concerned with good and evil. His or her superior is supposed to deal with these matters. Now we only need to be concerned about whether we are doing a good job. "Good" is of course defined by the organization. It is no longer defined by the individual's values.

In Nazi Germany, the bureaucratic process was its moral code. It established the divide between good and evil. It set the victimized group apart as a separate bureaucratic category. This act assured those not so categorized that they were immune from whatever might happen to the victimized group. The bureaucracy established the process whereby Jews were dismissed from their jobs and their businesses expropriated. The bureaucracy removed the victimized group from sight. Out of sight, Jews were not encountered in everyday life. It became less likely that anyone would hear the stories of the marginalized Jews. Sympathy and empathy for these unseen victims became much less likely.[25]

Concentration completed this distancing process by removing the victims from society. They were no longer encountered. No particular Jewish person was known. The public knew the victimized group only through abstract categories, and Nazi propaganda supplied the content for these categories. Concentration camps made Nazi propaganda more difficult to resist. A German was unlikely to accept propaganda that claimed the Jews sub-human if he or she actually socialized with Jewish people. In Nazi Germany, the concentration of the Jews meant the absence of social contact; therefore, a Gentile would have no experience of a Jew to contradict Nazi propaganda. Absent the empirical evidence provided by every day association, propaganda was much more likely to be believed.[26] Exploitation and starvation further disguised the humanity of the victims who, emaciated by starvation and oppression, began to look as sub-human as the propaganda declared. After such inhuman treatment, annihilation did not appear to be such a great step at all. It is a simple "logical" outcome of a bureaucratic process begun by the moral task of weeding out the "evil" from the "good."

The Holocaust and Civilization

The Holocaust is the most terrible and extreme example of the death-dealing consequences of civilization and its morality. It was not inevitable. It did not have to happen. It might have been prevented if someone other than Adolph Hitler had assumed absolute power in one of the most modern, technologically advanced, bureaucratic, civilized states in the world. The goals of the Holocaust, however, were not too different from other civilized attempts to destroy people deemed inferior.

In the case of the American Indian population, for example, Euro-Americans defined the Indians as uncivilized vermin. Euro-Americans expropriated Indian lands and profaned Indian religious places. The conquerors destroyed Indian livelihood by removing them from their native lands and slaughtering the animals Indians hunted for food. Indian men, women and children were killed either by violent acts or disease. Their population was concentrated on reservations where poverty, starvation, disease and death were all too common.[27] In other words a plan similar to the one Hilberg discovered in the Holocaust was present in American attempts to eliminate its undesirables.

Definition

Expropriation of Land

Concentration

Impoverishment and Starvation

Annihilation

Perhaps the only difference between the Nazi Holocaust and the American attempts to destroy the American Indians is that the Nazi bureaucracies were far more scientific, technically competent and efficient. Both were civilized attempts to deal with excess or undesirable population.

Civilization's recent attempts at genocide are consistent with the processes begun in the agricultural revolution. Excess food created excess population. When food became a commodity, we developed criteria to determine who was worthy of food and who was not. These criteria rapidly became our morality. Morality continues to marginalize the ones deemed evil and justify the "good ones" whenever the "good ones" leave "the bad ones" for dead. More sophisticated moral tactics lead to hierarchy building. The existence of these social hierarchies often led to aggressive attacks on those who morality has marginalized. The Holocaust and other genocides have often been a consequence of such hierarchy building, and they demonstrate that these death-dealing tactics are not unusual. Indeed, they are regular occurrences that are consistent with the principles deep within civilization itself.

Chapter 5:

Ethics without Morality

"The knowledge of good and evil seems to be the aim of all ethical reflection. The first task of Christian ethics is to invalidate this knowledge."

Dietrich Bonheoffer[1]

Many people do not feel at home in the world because it feels like there is a rift between human beings and the world. This feeling is hardly universal, but it is not uncommon. Existentialist philosophers, for example, have found this rift so profound they use it as a starting point for their philosophical speculations. Since existentialists believe God is dead, they have no hope that this abyss between humanity and the world can be overcome. Their only hope is to live with it.

Hans Jonas – a pupil of the renowned existentialist philosopher Martin Heidegger – argues that this existentialist starting point is not exactly modern. Indeed, a belief in this rift between humanity and the world has remarkable affinities with an extremely influential school of thought developed in the Greco-Roman world of the first Christian centuries. Today, we call this school of thought Gnosticism.[2] Gnostics also thought human beings were aliens in this world. Whereas modern existentialists usually take this alienation as a given, Gnostics accounted for it with a creation myth that taught that creation was a mistake. Unbeknownst to the supreme God, a subordinate god (the demiurge) created the world. The demiurge did so by placing a life force or soul in each individual bit of matter. All living things in this world are individual instances of "besouled" matter. The Gnostics taught that the world is corrupt and evil because it was created out of matter. There is a rift between humanity and the world because human souls, which are immaterial and good, have been imprisoned in evil matter. Human beings will not be at home until our souls are freed from these material prisons. Like modern existentialist philosophers, the Gnostics also thought that the rift between humanity and the world cannot be overcome as long as we are in this world. Unlike the existentialists, the Gnostics believed liberation was a possibility. Right knowledge could free us from our plight. Each Gnostic school offered a gnosis (knowledge or teaching) of how a soul can unlock its material prison.

Western Christianity was greatly influenced by this idea. Since St. Augustine of Hippo (354-430 CE), Western Christians have nearly unanimously understood the Garden of Eden story as humanity's act of rebellion against God. We now call this story "The Story of the Fall." While Augustine's interpretation has some connection to the Apostle Paul and the New Testament, the Garden of Eden story was not interpreted as an out and out rebellion against God by Christians prior to Augustine. (Jews rarely if ever interpreted it this way). St. Irenaeus (fl 180-200 CE), for example, interpreted the Garden of Eden story more benignly. He did not think that Adam and Eve eating the forbidden fruit was an act of rebellion. Instead he thought it was more or less predictable given Adam and Eve's immaturity.[3] Adam and Eve were no more rebelling against God than are children rebelling against their parents when they meander away in a grocery store. It is just what children do.

When Augustine reinterpreted the Garden of Eden story as a story of rebellion against God, he created the same rift between humanity and the world that the Gnostics created with their creation myths. Because of St. Augustine's near monopoly on

Western Christian thinking, Western Christians and the Western world for that matter came to understand human beings as aliens in this world. We had been created for another world (the Garden of Eden), but we live as exiles in this one. Our sin or rebellion prevents us from ever going back to the world for which we were created and from which we had been exiled. In Augustine's view, Jesus overcomes this rift for us and allows us to return to a world for which we were truly created. Until the Kingdom of God comes, we will be alienated from the world we inhabit. Despite Jesus himself saying that the Kingdom of God is in our midst, Augustine's interpretation of The Fall dominates the Western psyche. It probably is the reason existentialist philosophers think as they do. The difference between Augustine and the existentialist is Augustine believed God's grace could liberate us from our alienated state. In the absence of God, the existentialists believe alienation is humanity's permanent condition.

Like Gnosticism, Christianity and existentialism, this book has also argued that there is a rift between humanity and the world. It agrees we are not at home in this world. However, it has stated the reason for this rift in non-mythological terms. Following the work of Daniel Quinn and Jared Diamond, we have argued that this rift occurred in human history!! The Gnostics and Augustinian theology account for the rift in mythological terms in the sense that they think the rift happened before our current time. The existentialists believe this rift is an unavoidable fact of life that cannot be overcome. This book argues that the rift happened in history, and human actions contributed to the feeling that something is amiss. Specifically, the rift happened when the agricultural revolution commoditized food. The rift became more pronounced over time as the social, moral and intellectual consequences of the agricultural revolution's principle technology - the commoditization of food - became more pronounced. We have this development in the emergence of the dominator paradigm coupled with the diminution of the partnership paradigm. The fact of the matter is, however, *we created this rift!! It is therefore possible that we might be able to overcome it.*

The rift will not be overcome until its characteristics are articulated. Since morality is one way this rift is perpetuated, the first portion of this book was dedicated to exposing the death-dealing character of morality. The second portion of this book discusses an alternative. This chapter discusses ethics as an antidote to morality. The next chapter describes a number of ethical tactics or virtues. It will be argued that the practice of these ethical virtues do not merely lay the groundwork for overcoming the rift, they often eliminate the rift itself. The practice of these virtues and tactics make partnership ways an immediate reality which lasts as long as ethical virtues and tactics are practiced.

How Ethics Differs from Morality

It is difficult to distinguish between ethics and morality because we are trained to think of them as the same. Nevertheless many scholars have found this a useful distinction to make. Latin American Liberation theologian Enrique Dussell was the first person I encountered to do so, but he is not alone. Post-modern philosophers like Emmanuel Levinas and Zygmunt Bauman make similar distinctions. In their book *Comparative Religious Ethics,* Danniel Fasching and Dell Dechant also note differences between ethics and morality.[4] Chilean biologist/philosopher Humberto Maturana even calls for "ethics without morality."[5] The next chapters are in accord with Maturana's agenda. Their purpose is to develop an ethics without morality.

Morality and ethics differ because morality supports civilization and ethics supports life. Morality's support for civilization has already been demonstrated. It draws the line between good and evil. It grants divine sanction to this arbitrary division. Then it orders the civilization in accord with its understanding of good and evil, and rationalizes the social order. It establishes a social hierarchy that places the best at the apex and orders others according to how closely they approach the goodness of the apex. Actions and entities are deemed "good" or "moral" to the extent that they conform to that which is found at the apex of civilization. Ethics is different because it supports life instead of civilization. This chapter and the next discuss how ethics supports life. For now it is important to note that ethical activities differ from moral activities because supporting life is not the same thing as supporting civilization. Whereas the knowledge of good and evil is fundamental to the practice of morality, ethics seeks to invalidate this knowledge.[6]

The most fundamental distinction between ethics and morality is that ethics does not distinguish between good and evil, and it rejects what morality claims to be good. Instead, ethics is governed by the needs of those marginalized by morality. Enrique Dussel gives the following formidable insight.

> The ethical is not governed by moral norms – by what the system proclaims to be good. The ethical is governed by what the poor require. . . . Thus the ethical transcends the moral. *Moral systems are relative.* Latin American history has witnessed the Aztec, the colonial and the capitalist morality. Each of these systems has sought to legitimate the praxis of domination as good; each in its own way. *Ethics by contrast, is one and absolute, valid in every situation and every age.*[7]

Morality justifies whatever system of social hierarchy the dominator system provides. When the political system takes the form of patriarchy, morality will justify men. When it is a monarchy, morality will tell you kings are gods, or they rule by divine right. When the dominator system is capitalistic, its morality justifies private property and those who acquire great wealth with theories like Social Darwinism, or the Protestant Work Ethic. Morality stands ready to justify any political system from fascism to democracy. It has been doing this since the dawn of civilization when morality developed the criteria that determined a person's worthiness to receive food.

Ethics does not serve civilization. It supports life. Its function is always the same. *It always identifies with those marginalized by the morality of any social system.* A feudalistic system uses morality to justify the feudal order while an ethical person would identify with people marginalized by the morality of the feudal order – the serfs and peasants. Capitalist morality justifies private property and the rich while an ethical person within a capitalistic system identifies with the poor and homeless. In a meritocracy, morality justifies the meritorious while an ethical person considers those without merit. Nazi morality justified the Aryans whereas an ethical person in Nazi Germany would identify with the Jews. Since ethics is reasoned activity in the service of life, ethical people will also identify with non-human life forms if these life forms are marginalized or not given due consideration by the civilized ones. Thus, ethics can identify with other species, the environment and even the earth when our policies and practices marginalize these life forms.

Identification is the opposite of what we have called definition. As we have seen, definition was the first step in Nazi tyranny. The Jews, and others the Nazis deemed inferior, were defined then isolated. Identification does not allow definition of that sort to happen. During World War II, the way the Danes protected Danish Jews from the Holocaust is a profound, historical illustration of identification. As noted in our discussion of the Holocaust, the Nazis reinforced their definition of the Jews by making them wear the Star of David badge. The Danish government subverted this policy in an ethical, life-giving manner. They did not return evil for Nazi evil as most people who resisted Nazi tyranny did. They were different. Upon being presented with the Nazi plan to make the 7800 Danish Jews wear the Star of David badge, the Danish King, in identification with the Jews, told the Nazis that this was such a good idea that all Danes would wear the badge! Indeed, the royal family would be the first to don the attire. In addition, the entire Danish government threatened to resign if any anti-Jewish measures were instituted. Nazi reign depended on the cooperation of local officials. Indeed, the Nazis received such cooperation everywhere but Denmark. The courageous Danish response prevented the Nazis from introducing their death-dealing version of the moral divide. The Star of David badge was never worn by Danish Jews. Absent the badge, there was no visible distinction between a Jew and a non-Jew. The Jews could not be defined. They could not be placed on the "evil" side of the moral divide. Denmark subverted Nazi policy.[8]

The story does not end there. The Germans were on the defensive in August, 1943. Riots occurred. Danish shipyards and dockworkers refused to service German ships. General von Hanneken, the military governor of Denmark, imposed marshal law. Himmler and the S.S. thought marshal law provided the opportunity to settle the "Jewish question" in Denmark. The S.S. sought the help of the military. Astonishingly, General von Hanneken refused to place his troops at the disposal of the S.S. The S.S. had to import German police to seize the Danish Jews. Before these raids took place, however, German military authorities in Denmark informed the German police that they would not be allowed to break into Jewish dwellings. Such actions, they were told, were illegal and would create conflict with the Danish police. The German police were only authorized to knock on the door and seize those unfortunate enough to open their doors.[9]

To complicate the Nazi task further, nearly everyone knew the Germans were coming.

> On the morning of Friday, September 30, 1943, Rabbi Marcus Melchior stood before the Holy Ark of the 110 year-old Copenhagen Synagogue. It was the day before Rosh Hashanah, the Jewish New Year. About 150 members of the congregation were present. They were puzzled by the fact that Rabbi Melchior was not in his rabbinical robes.
>
> "There will be no service this morning," said Rabbi Melchior. "Instead, I have very important news to tell you. Last night I received word that tomorrow the Germans plan to raid Jewish homes throughout Copenhagen to arrest all the Danish Jews for shipment to concentration camps. They know that tomorrow is Rosh Hashanah and our families will be home. The situation is very serious. We must take action immediately. You must leave the synagogue now and contact all relatives, friends and neighbors you know who are Jewish and tell them what I have told you. You must tell them to pass the word on to everyone they know is Jewish. You must also speak to all your Christian friends and tell them to warn the Jews. You must do this immediately, within the next few minutes, so that two or three hours from now everyone will know what is happening. By nightfall tonight we must all be in hiding."[10]

The Danish Jews went into hiding. They had plenty of places to hide because all Danes stood ready to receive them. The Germans found only 477 out of 7800 people that evening.[11] Ultimately the Danes enabled the Jews they sheltered that night to reach safety in Sweden, and the Danish government kept track of the Jews who were captured by the Germans that night. As a result, a vast majority of the 477 Jews captured that night survived the Holocaust.

Most people believe the only way to resist a force as diabolical as Nazi Germany would be to adopt Nazi tactics. The Danes, however, resisted the most infamous and death-dealing Nazi program without adopting the Nazi tactics of terror. The Danes responded ethically. They *identified with* and supported their Jewish neighbors. They succeeded because they rejected the Nazi version of morality. In refusing to make Danish Jews wear the Star of David badge, they rejected the Nazi version of morality that drew the moral divide between the "good" Aryan and the "evil" Jew. This stopped a more complex classification of Jews the Nazis imposed elsewhere and prevented the Danish Jews from entering the death-dealing German bureaucratic process.

The Danish resistance did not simply prevent the Nazi tactics of terror. This story also suggests Danish actions may have *created* something as well. Danish resistance enabled an alternative community to develop. This community saved the lives of many Jews who were marginalized by Nazi tyranny. Moreover, the mere experience of this alternative community may have enabled hardened Germans to understand life differently. This different understanding may be the reason that General von Hanneken refused to place his soldiers at the disposal of the S.S It may also have been the reason that he limited the power of the German police imported from Germany to arrest the Danish Jews. Obviously, there is no way we can know for sure, but what we do know is that von Hanneken's actions were unusual. Perhaps these unusual actions were a consequence of the fact that, absent the Star of David badge, the occupation forces were not easily able to isolate and define the Jews. Perhaps they actually experienced alternatives to Nazi domination. Maybe this led them to assist the Danes in their protection of the Jews. We will never know the truth of this matter, but this is clearly one way to interpret these events.

Jesus was not Moral (He was Ethical)

Jesus is the most misinterpreted person in history because Christians tend to believe that Jesus supports civilization and the dominator system. Nothing could be further from the truth. The agents of civilization executed him. Like the Holocaust, Jesus' execution was not a moral malfunction on the part of those who executed him. His was a legal execution. It had morality on its side. The religious authorities turned him over to the political authorities and, religious and political leadership of Jesus' day combined to execute him in accord with the laws of the land. Most Christians would have us forget this. The church is ordered hierarchically. It preaches morality, and, in general, the church has lent its support to nearly every government established in the Western world and every war fought by the nations of the Western world. Despite the claims of most Christians, however, Jesus was not moral. Jesus was ethical. He would have stood for none of this.

The Good Samaritan story is remarkably consistent with the distinction being made between morality and ethics. For those who only know the Good Samaritan to be the name of a local hospital, the story will be told. Jesus was approached by a teacher of the law. The law this teacher taught was not constitutional law or corporate law. The law this teacher taught was the Torah. The Torah is the first five books of the Hebrew Bible. The teacher of the law was a person who tried to apply the laws found in the Torah to everyday life. He was engaged in morality. The knowledge of good and evil was important to him.

The teacher asked Jesus a religious question. To those be-witched by the dominator system, the teacher's question might be considered the most important religious question. He asked what he must do to receive eternal life. Jesus did not answer his question. Instead Jesus asked a question himself, "What do Scriptures (the Torah) say? How do you interpret them?" (Luke 10: 26). The teacher of the law replied, "Love the Lord your God with all your heart, with all your soul, with all your strength and with all your mind and love your neighbor as yourself." (Luke 10: 27). Jesus told him that he was right. Jesus probably would have left it at that, but the teacher needed more clarification.

Apparently the teacher of the law did not have a problem loving God with all his heart, but he was not so sure about the neighbor part. The story tells us that "in an effort to *justify* himself, the teacher asked, 'Who is my neighbor?'" The teacher could have been thinking that if he could just get Jesus to define neighbor (remember definition is the first step in both morality and marginalization), then loving one's neighbor would be a little easier. The teacher was searching for definition. If Jesus would just tell him that these people are neighbors and those people are not, then the teacher could go about the business of loving those designated neighbors and marginalizing those who were not so designated.

The teacher was inviting Jesus to take the first step in the moral process, namely, to draw the moral divide between neighbor and non-neighbor. What is significant about the Good Samaritan story is that Jesus did not draw the moral divide. He refused to address the teacher's question in a moral context. Instead, Jesus told the following story:

> A man was going down from Jerusalem to Jericho, and he fell among robbers, who stripped him and beat him, and departed leaving him half dead. Now by chance a priest was going down the road, and when he saw him, he passed by on the other side. So likewise, a Levite, when he came to the place and saw him, passed by on the other side. But a Samaritan, as he journeyed, came to where he was; and when he saw him, he had compassion and went to him and bound up his wounds, putting on oil and wine; then he set him on his own beast and brought him to an inn, and took care of him. And the next day he took out two denarii gave them to the innkeeper, saying, 'Take care of him, and whatever more you spend, I will repay you when I come back. (Jesus asked the teacher) 'Which of these, do you think proved neighbor to the man who fell among robbers?' (The teacher) said, 'The one who showed mercy on him.' Jesus said to him, 'Go and do likewise.' (Luke 10: 30-37).

In Christian circles this is a familiar story, but this familiarity prevents us from appreciating its radical character. In this day and age we routinely call someone who performs a good deed a

"Good Samaritan." We believe the words "good" and "Samaritan" belong together. A first century Palestinian Jew – the ones to whom Jesus told this story - would make no such connection. The Samaritans were the enemy. They were heretics. They were a religious and social threat. The word good would never be used as an adjective to modify Samaritan in any sentence uttered by a first century Palestinian Jew. This would be like a patriotic American Christian telling a story about a friendly Islamic terrorist with a great sense of humor.

The teacher of the law would expect the priest or the Levite to act as neighbor. It never would have occurred to him that the hated Samaritan could be a neighbor. Samaritans were the obvious non-neighbor. Any Jew who drew the moral divide would have drawn it in such a way that the Samaritans would be found on the "evil" side of the moral divide. When Jesus asked the teacher to tell him who proved to be the neighbor to the man who fell among thieves, the teacher could not even bring himself to say the Samaritan was the neighbor. The force of his moral beliefs may have been too powerful for him to utter the words "Samaritan" and "neighbor" in the same sentence. Instead, he said that the one who *showed mercy* is the neighbor. In the context of our discussion concerning ethics, there is no more significant admission than this.

Mercy is an ethical virtue because mercy makes no distinction between the worthy ones and the unworthy ones. An act of mercy renounces the moral divide. Mercy disregards any distinction between good and evil. In undermining the Nazi attempt to separate the "good" Aryans from the "evil" Jews, the Danes acted mercifully. Likewise, the Samaritan acted mercifully because he ignored the moral divide separating the Jews from the Samaritans. Samaritans, after all, felt the same about the Jews as the Jews felt about them. *Since the neighbor is the one who shows mercy, the neighbor is a person who does not live in accord with moral dictates that leave people for dead.* The neighbor disregards such demarcations. The one who shows mercy refuses to have his or her behavior dictated by a person's rank in society. The neighbor will simply try to meet the needs of the other.

The Parable of the Laborers in the Vineyard dramatically illustrates how an act of mercy undermines the way morality normally functions. The parable begins with the words, "The Rule of God is like this." The parable proceeds to establish a sharp contrast between morality and God's ethical rule.

> The rule of God is like a householder who went out early in the morning to hire laborers for his vineyard. After agreeing with the laborers for a denarius a day, he sent them into his vineyard. And going out about the third hour he saw others standing idle in the market place; and to them he said, "You go into the vineyard too, and whatever is right I will give you." So they went. Going out again about the sixth hour and the ninth hour he went out and found others standing; and he said to them, "Why do you stand here idle all day?" They said to him, "Because no one has hired us." He said to them, "You go into the vineyard too." And when evening came, the owner of the vineyard said to his steward, "Call the laborers and pay them their wages, beginning with the last, up to the first." And when those hired about the eleventh hour came, each of them received a denarius. Now when the first came, they thought they would receive more; but each of them also received a denarius. And on receiving it they grumbled at the householder saying, "These last worked only one hour, and you have made them equal to us who have borne the burden of the day and the scorching heat." But he replied to one of them, "Friend, I am doing you no wrong; did you not agree with me for a denarius? Take what belongs to you and go; I choose to give to this last as I give to you. Am I not allowed to do what I choose with what belongs to me? Or do you begrudge my generosity?" (Mt 20: 1-14).

Nearly everyone thinks that there is something quite wrong with the owner's behavior in this parable. True, he did meet his contractual obligations. He paid those who had worked the entire day the agreed upon amount. Yet, nearly everyone thinks some kind of injustice has been done in this parable.

The story is made even more disagreeable because the owner could have avoided the conflict if he had just paid those who had worked all day first. They could have been sent home, and then he could have given those who did not work the entire day whatever he pleased. The owner does not even take this route. As a matter of fact, he deliberately paid those who had worked fewer hours before he paid those who had worked all day. He appears to have wanted those who had worked the longest to *see* that he was paying the latecomers the same amount they would receive.

The reason almost everyone thinks that there is something wrong here is that we and the laborers who had worked all day prefer morality to mercy. It is our preference for ranking that tells us that something is amiss in this story. Ranking tells us that those who work longer hours are more worthy than those who do not work as long. Our moral code demands that the ones who work longer receive higher status and more money. The owner does not operate according to this moral code. Instead of giving what was "earned," he gives what was needed; for it is generally thought that one denarius was the amount of money a Palestinian family needed to make it through the day. In giving what was needed rather than what was deserved, the owner was acting in accord with "the rule of God." He showed mercy, and thereby, rejected the merciless morality that plagues the marginalized.

This parable reveals our resistance to mercy. We resist because we do not think we need mercy. Morality creates the illusion that we do not need mercy by suggesting that a person's moral worth is within a person's control; hence, those on the good side of the moral divide will resent the unworthy ones when they receive grace and mercy. The unworthy ones are supposed to earn their status! This is how morality cultivates its allies. Mercy and grace are rarely thought desirable by people who consider themselves morally worthy. Such people believe they owe their success to hard work or some other action or quality. They do not believe there is a relationship between their success and mercy or grace. Accordingly, they do not like mercy and grace because mercy and grace undermine the privileges of rank and morality.

This is true in all spheres of life controlled by the dominator system. Religious people who think they have made themselves worthy by virtue of their prayers, mature spiritual life or generosity have great difficulty with a merciful God. Like those in the parable who have borne the heat of the day, they cannot help but wonder why they have done all they have done if God grants mercy to those less worthy than they. They do not care if other people live or die. They only care that the rules are followed. They think justice demands that they receive more than those who have accomplished less. This is not just a religious or economic issue. It is the issue surrounding immigrants we Americans call "illegal aliens." These people are "illegal!" They have not followed the rules. Showing mercy (we call it amnesty) is anathema to those in bondage to morality and the dominator system.

Jesus opposes morality in another way. He never answers a moral question in a direct, unambiguous way. In the Good Samaritan story, Jesus did not define neighbor as requested. Instead he told the Good Samaritan story, and the teacher of the law, not Jesus, said the one who showed mercy was the one who acted as neighbor. Elsewhere Jesus was asked one of the most important moral questions of his day, namely, whether taxes should be paid. The Herodian party said that taxes to Rome should be paid. The Pharisees thought otherwise. The argument was constant, and the Pharisees and Herodians often bitterly disputed this moral concern. Jesus had a way of uniting enemies, and apparently he united the Herodians and the Pharisees. Unfortunately, he united these powerful groups against himself. Matthew 23:15-22 relates an event in which these two parties tried to trap Jesus. They asked Jesus if taxes to Romans should be paid. They wanted a simple yes or no. They got something quite different. Jesus asked them to show him a coin. He asked whose face was on the coin. When he was told that it was the Emperor's face, Jesus told them to "render unto Caesar the things that are Caesar's and to God the things that are God's." In short, Jesus did not answer the question!

Jesus' response did two things. First, it recognized that there actually is a difference between political authorities and God. Our civilizations want us to forget this distinction. The union between political and religious authorities makes it appear that the man-made rules that establish morality and justify ranking are god-given. Sometimes civilization and the dominator system achieve this union by claiming the political rulers are in fact God. Egyptian Pharaohs made this claim. The Roman Emperor Domitian made this claim. He demanded that he be addressed by the title *Deus et dominus noster Domitianus* (Our Lord and God

Domitian).[12] Under Christian influence, Western monarchs reluctantly recognized the distinction between themselves and God, but the close relationship between themselves and gods persisted. The Pope crowned Charlemagne Holy Roman Emperor. England's Henry VIII was declared defender of the faith. Theories of the divine rights of kings emerged. Today these connections remain whenever political leaders claim they have special conversations with the deity. Political authority and religious authority are always linked. Jesus denies this link when he suggests there is a difference between Caesar and God.

Second, Jesus' response demands that his questioners determine the relationship between God and government for themselves. Ironically, this was the exact problem everyone wanted him to remove when they asked their question. Jesus refused to answer this and other moral questions because doing so would have made him moral. Answering a moral question draws the moral divide. If Jesus said taxes *should* be paid, then those who refuse to pay taxes would be judged immoral. If he had said taxes *should not* be paid, then those who pay taxes are consigned to the evil side of the moral divide. Since Jesus refused to answer, he did not draw the moral divide. He did not label anyone good or evil, clean or unclean, moral or immoral, saved or damned, saint or sinner, worthy or unworthy. Jesus left it to others (individuals or communities) to decide when and if taxes should be paid. Perhaps the question remains open because sometimes taxes should be paid and sometimes not.

Jesus was not moral. He was ethical. Jesus was ethical instead of moral because he rejected morality's death-dealing function and supported life instead. He refused to draw the line separating the good from the bad or the clean from the unclean. Jesus was ethical because he identified with those marginalized and left for dead by his culture's moral system. In a culture that marginalized the sick by calling them unclean and literally untouchable, Jesus healed the sick with a touch. In a culture that despised tax collectors calling them traitors and extortionists, Jesus ate with tax collectors. He even made one or two his disciples. Jesus always crossed the moral divide. He even asked God to forgive his executioners!

In recent years, many people courageously identify with the poor, the hungry and others who are socially marginalized. In the process, some have suffered and others have given their lives. Nevertheless, most of these courageous people remain subject to morality and the dominator system because they redrew the moral divide. Their courageous identification with the poor and the marginalized led them to place the poor and powerless on the good side of the moral divide and the rich and powerful on the evil side. In short, they still drew the moral divide and divided people into the good guys and the bad guys. What is interesting about Jesus is that he did not redraw the moral divide. He remained in association with the Pharisees. He spoke to his religious critics. He even ate with them as he ate with the tax collectors and sinners. Jesus apparently had no agenda in meeting these people other than fellowship and conversation. In short, Jesus did what he preached others should do. He loved his enemies. This of course does not mean that Jesus liked his enemies. It means he refused to dehumanize them. He could listen to them even when he was not being heard by them. He disregarded the moral divide altogether.

Jesus Refused the Moral Divide?

Students of the New Testament might object to the statement that Jesus never made moral distinctions. The argument that follows suggests that Jesus clearly made distinctions, but they were not moral distinctions. It is quite possible that we think the distinctions Jesus made were moral distinctions because *we* are bewitched by the dominator system, and, as a consequence, we are likely to interpret most any distinction as a moral distinction. Morality is our worldview. We interpret everything in terms of good and evil. When Jesus separates the sheep from the goats in Matthew 25: 32, our moral worldview demands that sheep are good and that goats are evil. As difficult as it is for us to imagine, there might not be a moral difference between a sheep and a goat! Jesus might not be making a moral distinction at all. When Jesus calls the Pharisees hypocrites, a moral worldview would take the next step and conclude that hypocrites are unworthy and non-hypocrites are worthy. Jesus, on the other hand, may simply be describing the Pharisees. We may be the ones who assume a hypocrite is morally inferior to a non-hypocrite.

Matthew 13: 24-30 is one place where we often understand Jesus to be making moral distinctions. Distinctions are
indeed being made, but they are not necessarily moral distinctions.

> The Kingdom of heaven may be compared to
> someone who sowed good seed in his field, but
> while everyone . . . was asleep, an enemy came
> and sowed weeds among the wheat. So when the
> plants came up and bore grain, then the weeds
> appeared as well. And the slaves of the house-
> holder came and said to him, 'Master, did you not
> sow good seed in your field? Where, then, did
> these weeds come from?' He answered, 'An en-
> emy has done this!' The slaves said to him, 'Then
> do you want us to go and gather them?' But he
> replied, 'No, for in gathering the weeds you would
> uproot the wheat along with them. Let both of
> them grow together until the harvest; and at har-
> vest time I will tell the reapers, 'Collect the weeds
> first and bind them in bundles to be burned, but
> gather the wheat into my barn.' (Mt. 13: 24-30).

Obviously Jesus is making distinctions and separations
here, but these are not necessarily moral distinctions.[13] As a matter
of fact, when the householder's slave asks if the householder
wants the weeds pulled, the slave may be asking for a moral
distinction to be made between the good seed and the evil weeds.
The householder, however, tells him not to do this. The
householder tells him to wait until harvest time when the wheat
will be taken into the barn and the weeds bundled up to be burned.

Once again a moral interpretation might speculate that
Jesus is now drawing the moral divide. This could be the case if
being burned is the same thing as going to hell. This, however,
disregards the common practice of farmers putting all their
resources to the best use. It is actually more probable that the
weeds are being bundled to be burned for fuel instead of being
burned in hell. If so, the householder uses that which was planted
with evil intent to benefit the life of the household. He was able to
do this precisely because he did not separate the "good" seed from
the "evil" weeds as his slave had asked.

We seldom note that the word "weed" is an interpretation. What is a weed to one person is an important plant or flower to another. As a matter of fact, *a weed is probably more natural or indigenous to a particular place than the crop that is being planted!* In any case, gardening – which includes the forcible removal of weeds so that the "good" plants might prosper – was a metaphor used in the German Holocaust. The "evil' Jews were to be weeded out so that the "good' Aryans might have living space.

> Modern genocide is an element of social engineer-
> ing, meant to bring about a social order conform-
> ing to the design of the perfect society. . . This is
> a gardener's vision projected upon a world-size
> screen. The thoughts, feelings, dreams and drives
> of the designers of the perfect world are familiar
> to every gardener worth his name. . . . Some gar-
> deners hate the weeds that spoil their design. . . .
> others are quite unemotional about them; just a
> problem to be solved. . . . Not that it makes a dif-
> ference to the weeds (what sort of) gardeners ex-
> terminate them.[14]

In refusing to pull the weeds, the householder in the par-able may have recognized two important things. First, human beings determine what weeds are and what they are not. Moreover, when the gardening metaphor is extended to people, the weeds always correspond to the marginalized. Second, if this interpretation is reasonable, the householder recognized that even that which is called a weed has a life-giving purpose. This recognition prevented the householder from adopting the gardener metaphor. Accordingly, life was enhanced rather than diminished.

The greatest challenge to the claim that Jesus refused to draw the moral divide is Matthew 25: 31-45:

> When the Son of Man comes in his glory, and all
> the angels with him, then he will sit on his glori-
> ous throne. Before him will be gathered all the
> nations, and he will separate them one from an-
> other as a shepherd separates the sheep from the
> goats, and he will place the sheep at his right
> hand, but the goats at the left. Then the King will
> say to those at his right hand, "Come, O blessed of

my Father, inherit the kingdom prepared for you from the foundation of the world; for I was hungry and you gave me food, I was thirsty and you gave me drink, I was a stranger and you welcomed me, I was naked and you clothed me, I was sick and you visited me, I was in prison and you came to me." Then the righteous will answer him, "Lord, when did we see thee hungry and feed thee, or thirsty and give thee drink? And when did we see thee as stranger and welcome thee, or naked and clothe thee? And when did we see thee sick or in prison and visit thee?" And the King will answer them, "Truly I say to you, as you did it to one of the least of these my brethren, you did it to me." Then he will say to those at his left hand, "Depart from me, you cursed, into the eternal fire prepared for the devil and his angels; for I was hungry and you gave me no food, I was thirsty and you gave me no drink, I was a stranger and you did not welcome me, naked and you did not clothe me, sick and in prison and you did not visit me." Then they also will answer, "Lord, when did we see thee hungry or thirsty or a stranger or naked or sick or in prison and did not minister to thee?" Then he will answer them, "Truly, I say to you, as you did it not to one of the least of these, you did it not to me." And they will go away into eternal punishment and the righteous to eternal life. (Mt. 25: 31-46).

Distinctions are clearly being made here. One group goes to eternal life and the other to eternal punishment. This certainly sounds like the moral divide is established in accord with how the least of these are treated. Those who treat "the least of these" well are on the good side of the moral divide. Those who treat them poorly are assigned the evil side. Morality and hierarchy are maintained.

This passage, however, can be interpreted in a way that is slightly more in accord with partnership ways. The first thing to note is all the *nations* (not individuals) are gathered and judged in accord with how they treat the marginalized or "the least of these."

The question is, "Who are the 'least of these' and from where do they come?" In terms of our discussion, "the least of these" exist because of morality's universal function, namely, the marginalization of those a given civilization deems evil. In other words, what is being condemned here is morality and the dominator system. We have argued that ranking is the dominator system's definitive feature. Morality rationalizes the ranking process by establishing the moral divide. Moral criteria that establish the moral divide differ from place to place, but the function of morality always is the same. Morality always marginalizes someone. It always leaves someone for dead. In short, morality creates "the least of these" in all dominator civilizations it serves.

In this text Jesus is judging the *nations* (not the individual persons) of the world according to how they treat "the least of these." Since "the least of these" are a creation of morality and the dominator system, he is judging whether or not political entities like nations serve the dominator system!! Nations that live in accord with the dominator system rationalize poverty and marginalization. They may not even acknowledge the existence of poverty. Since they justify their treatment of the marginalized or "least of these," they often do not even know they treat the marginalized in life threatening ways. Such a nation, to use a farfetched example, might consider itself the greatest nation in the world yet deny its citizens health care, decent food, quality higher education, social security and living wages because unnecessary wars make these projects too expensive. A civilized nation like that would be very surprised at Jesus' judgment. Its leadership would in fact respond, "Lord, when did we see you hungry or thirsty or naked or sick or in prison and did not minister to you?" Such marginalization, however, is routine in civilized nations. We do not even know we are doing it because our morality justifies the practice of marginalization.

Nations that live in accord with partnership ways do not have starvation in the midst of plenty. When one starves, all starve. When there is plenty, everyone eats. Their culture is ordered in such a way that they do not even know that they aid "the least of these." They too might not remember treating the least of these favorably because such favorable treatment is routine. A distinction being recognized here, but it is a distinction already created by the dominator system itself. The dominator system is an agent of death to those it marginalizes. Jesus' response is in service of life. He is judging the nations only in the sense that he is exposing them for what they already are. There is an important difference between a moral distinction and a description of reality. It is a distinction that is not obvious, but can be drawn. In this instance, Jesus is describing social reality and saying that one way is not consistent with life. In fact, this way leads to death. His critique is based on what sort of nation a particular nation already is. Does the particular nation conform to a dominator society, or does it live in accord with partnership ways? Jesus favors partnership and life.

Finally, Jesus' crucifixion symbolizes both morality's rejection of Jesus and Jesus' rejection of morality. According to Martin Hengel, crucifixion was an execution reserved for the oppressed and the religious outcasts. The Romans understood crucifixion as the supreme death penalty. Lesser penalties included decapitation, burning at the stake, being fed to the lions or being swiftly run through with a sword.[15] Crimes meriting crucifixion included: desertion to the enemy, betraying secrets, incitement to rebellion, murder, prophecy about the welfare of the rulers, nocturnal impiety, magic and serious falsification of wills.[16] Due to its terrible nature, however, crucifixion was normally inflicted upon lower classes. Higher classes could expect more "humane" executions.

Crucifixion rapidly became the typical execution for slaves. It was even called "the slaves' punishment," and it was used to deter slave rebellion.[17] Since slaves were property and had few if any rights, slave rebellion could be interpreted rather loosely. Indeed, any form of disobedience or perceived laziness could be called rebellion as indicated by the following dialogue from a play by Juvenal.

> "Crucify that slave," says the wife. "But what crime worthy of death has he committed?" asks the husband. "Where are the witnesses? Who informed against him? Give him a hearing at least. No delay can be too long when a man's life is at stake." "What a fool you are!" (says the wife). "Do you call a slave a man? Do you say he has done no wrong? This is my will and my command: take it as authority for the deed."[18]

A Roman slave knew that his life was in the hands of another. A slave knew that she did not control her own destiny. Thus, the life of a slave symbolizes the lives of the world's poor and marginalized who also live without the illusion of mastery and control. Robbed of this illusion, survival becomes a conscious issue in the lives of the marginalized.

For the Romans, crucifixion was the slaves' death. Anyone who died on the cross died in solidarity with the marginalized of society. The Jewish understanding of the cross took this marginalization a step further. The Pharisaic interpretation of Deuteronomy 21: 22, 23 stated that if a person was crucified, he or she died cursed by God. Accordingly, such a person died cut off from the covenant. St. Paul summarized this position – a view he held before his conversion – in Galatians 3: 13. "Christ redeemed us from the curse of the law by becoming a curse for us – for it is written 'Cursed is anyone who hangs on a tree.'" In other words, the Torah itself states that Jesus did not just die a criminal's death. He died outside of the covenant. He died bereft of all forms of human decency. From the perspective of Jewish law, Jesus' crucifixion made him immoral. He died on the "evil" side of the moral divide. His last breath was taken far removed from the good, clean, worthy saints of the world.[19] Jesus' kenosis (self-emptying) not only includes Jesus emptying himself of his equality with God, but it also includes emptying himself of all forms of human decency. The things we take to constitute "the best of humanity" are abandoned on the cross. This is done in solidarity with the poor, the outcast, the immoral and the sinners. That is in solidarity with everyone on the evil side of the moral divide.

Martin Luther eloquently articulates this same theme in his commentary on the Galatians saying on the cross Jesus became "...the greatest thief, murderer, adulterer, robber, desecrator, blasphemer etc. *there had ever been anywhere in the world.*"[20] The cross is many things, but our service to morality and the dominator system often prevents us from understanding one of the most important aspects of the cross. The cross is the gallows. On the cross, Jesus abandons every privilege that morality and civilization might confer. By assuming the slave's death, Jesus abandoned the status social rank bestows. Moreover, on the cross Jesus rejected all claims to be morally superior. Indeed, he rejected moral goodness altogether. In the crucifixion, Jesus identified completely with the marginalized. *Jesus was legally executed by the state at the request of the religious authorities.* In other words, Jesus is left for dead by "good," respectable and powerful people of his day. It is not an unusual occurrence. Under the dominator system, with the justification of morality and the sanction of civilization, this happens to many others as well.

The Apostle Paul and the Moral Divide

The Apostle Paul was the first person to systematically attack the moral divide. In the first three chapters of Romans, Paul argues that the Gentiles (all people who are not Jews) have no excuse when they do not follow the Law because the Law of God can be clearly seen in nature (Rom. 1:18-32).[21] After thoroughly discussing the Gentiles, Paul discussed the Jews. He said they were explicitly given the Law, but they too violate it when they held themselves as examples for all to follow. Paul thought this made the Jews idolaters because they were substituting themselves for God. (Rom 2: 17-24). Since all human beings are either Jews or Gentiles, and since Paul thought both Jew and Gentile have fallen short of doing what the Law requires, Paul concluded the Law of Moses does not make anyone righteous or good.

> No one is righteous, no one:
>
> No one understands, no one seeks for God.
>
> All have turned aside, together they have gone wrong;
>
> No one does good, not even one. (Rom. 3: 10-12).

In a peculiar way, Paul's argument drives a wedge between religion and morality. Under the dominator system, morality always finds an ally in religion. Religion grants divine sanction to morality's separation of the good and the evil, the worthy and the unworthy, the saints and the sinners. For Paul, however, no one is righteous, good or worthy. If there is a moral divide, no one is on its "good" side. Morality cannot separate the good and worthy from the evil and unworthy because everyone is unworthy according to Paul.

Because those in the grasp of the dominator system understand the world from a moral perspective, we think that Paul is pessimistic about humanity's ability to do good. We discard his teaching on this subject, or refuse to remember it because we can cite instance after instance of people doing good things. Paul cannot be correct, we argue, because there is good in so many people.[22] Paul's argument, however, can just as easily be understood as an attack on morality itself. If everyone is on the evil side of the moral divide, no one can be marginalized. Morality's death-dealing function – its ability to marginalize – is destroyed.[23]

Abandoning the moral divide enabled Paul to abandon hierarchy-building as well. Paul clearly understood the community called church in non-hierarchical ways. Logic compelled him to understand the church non-hierarchically because his rejection of the moral divide deprived him of the criteria necessary to make the distinctions that lead to hierarchy. Instead, Paul envisioned non-hierarchical forms of organization. He thought of the church organically. He called it the Body of Christ and noted that one organ of the body was just as vital as any other (I Cor. 12: 4-30). Moreover, Paul eliminated the political, sexual and religious distinctions often used to establish hierarchy. In the church "there is no longer Jew or Gentile, there is no longer slave or free, there is no longer male or female; for all of you are one in Christ Jesus" (Gal. 3: 28). Implicit in Paul's efforts to envision alternative communities, however, is the tragic fact that these communities had to be created in the first place. Biblical communities are always established as an alternative to the dominator model. They must be created almost from nothing. It is a daunting task.

Post-Modern Ethics

Efforts to distinguish between ethics and morality are not limited to Christian theologians. Two post-modern ethicists, Emmanuel Levinas and Zygmunt Bauman, make such distinctions.

The names post-modern and modern can be misleading. They do not refer to two historical eras where the era called modern is followed by the era called post-modern. The names are a consequence of the fact that the post-modernism rejects modernism. Thus, the post-modern depends on the modern. Post-modernism would not exist if modernism did not exist; however, both exist simultaneously.

In so far as ethics and morality are concerned, the debate between modernism and post-modernism can be summarized as follows. Proponents of modernism believe that a universal moral code exists. This moral code applies to all people at all times and in all situations. Proponents of modernism either believe this moral code is known and needs to be implemented, or they think it has not yet been discovered but soon will be.[24] Religious fundamentalists are modern because they believe this universal moral code exists. They know the code. They believe it is universally applicable, but most recognize that they do not now have the power to implement this code on a national or global level. By the same token, the very day this is being written, Pope Benedict has reasserted the supremacy of the Roman Catholic Church saying that it is the only true expression of the truth of the Gospel. This is evidence of the Pope's adherence to modernity. The underlying claim is, after all, that a true religion exists in Roman Catholicism, and it is the supreme expression of religious truth for all people for all time and in all places. The irony is non-Roman Catholic Christians disagree with His Holiness largely because they think *their* version of Christianity is the supreme expression of religious truth for all people at all times and in all places. They too are modern.

Modernity is not limited to religious circles. The inventors of modernity, the philosophers of the 17th and 18th century Enlightenment, also believed that there is a universal moral code. Ideological Marxists who believe a future classless society is inevitable are modern. Even our current economic doctrine of development and globalization is modern because it holds that one sort of economy, namely an extreme version of free market capitalism, should be universal.

Post-modern ethics rejects the modern contention that there is a universal moral code.[25] Contrary to popular belief, this does not mean that post-modernism is morally relative. Indeed, a radical understanding of ethical responsibility dominates post-modern ethics. Responsibility, however, is not grounded in a moral code. It is a consequence of a face-to-face encounter with "the other." We are infinitely responsible for "the other." This responsibility is not rationally deduced from a pre-established moral code as it might be in modernism. It is more radical. It has nothing to do with thought or intellectual speculation. *We are infinitely responsible for "the other" simply because "the other" exists.*[26]

In post-modern ethics, the relationship to "the other" is asymmetrical. We are simply responsible for "the other." No thing, no person or concept is more fundamental or basic than one's encounter with "the other." Our ethical responsibility is not based on "the other's" goodness or social position. Nothing is required of "the other." Disturbing, ungrateful behavior does not absolve us of our responsibility.[27] Our responsibility is not rational because it does not involve arguing from a metaphysical premise to a moral conclusion. Responsibility is the consequence of a face-to-face encounter alone.[28]

In an effort to overcome the rules, authorities, hierarchies and moral codes, some post-modern ethicists have made a remarkable and ingenious philosophical move. They have made ethics the first principle of reflection. They have made "the other" the point of departure for rational thought. Ethics is normally conceived as a rational process where a decision is rationally deduced from a metaphysical principle of some sort. A post-modern ethicist, on the other hand, begins reflection with his or her infinite responsibility for "the other." "The other" is the first principle of thought. In other words, "the other" holds the place that Being occupies in traditional metaphysics.

Traditional metaphysics describes Being and makes moral deductions based upon Being's attributes. For example, "Good" traditionally describes an attribute of Being. Since Being is "Good" and since Being is the source of all that is, a traditional metaphysician would argue that everything that exists has some good in it. A moral argument might proceed as follows: Since Being is good, our actions should conform to the goodness in Being; therefore, we should be good to others. Now clearly this argument is over simplified. The only point being made here is in traditional metaphysics, Being is the starting point of reflection. Every opinion about any matter other than Being is deduced from the qualities of Being itself. Morality involves deducing our need to act in accord with the Good from the contention that Being, the starting point of all reflection, is Good.

Post-modern ethics supplants the fundamental status of Being in traditional metaphysics. Instead, our infinite responsibility to "the other" is the starting point for all reflection. Ethics, not metaphysics, is the first philosophy, and the encounter with "the other" is fundamental. The encounter with "the other" is similar to acting mercifully toward "the other."[29]

The mention of mercy brings us back to the story of the Good Samaritan. This story has an interesting relationship to post-modern ethics. The Levite and priest who did not help the dying man probably had their reasons for passing. Some have speculated that they left the man for dead because of their moral code which said physical contact with a dead body made a person unclean. Those who had such contact had to go through a ritual cleansing process. Both of these guys were busy. They probably did not have time for the cleansing ritual. They were needed elsewhere. They may have reasoned this way, or they may have reasoned that stopping to help would make them vulnerable to the very thugs who tried to kill the guy in the ditch. Whatever their reasoning process was, *their reasoning process prevented them from assisting the one in need.* [30] In light of our current discussion of post-modern ethics, the priest and the Levite represent modernism. Their lack of aid was determined by a reasoning process that began with certain principles and ended with an action deduced from these principles.

Like the Levite and priest, the Samaritan could have justified leaving the victim for dead. This Samaritan did otherwise. He was neighbor to the dying man. He showed mercy. Accordingly, the Samaritan is an example of the post-modernist claim that we are infinitely responsible for the other. The Samaritan's responsibility was asymmetrical. He had no concern for compensation. He simply gave the man what was needed. Also in accord with post-modern ethics, the Samaritan's action was pre-rational. He did not reason from certain intellectual principles to the conclusion that the victim should be helped. His responsibility was the consequence of a face-to-face encounter. It was not derived from some moral argument.

The post-modern assertion that the other has absolute status appears to be very similar to the assertion that the neighbor is the one who shows mercy. There is, however, an important difference. An act of mercy is a specific sort of act. In agreement with post-modern ethicists, mercy disregards moral codes. The post-modern emphasis on the radical responsibility for "the other," however, completely disregards context. In post-modern ethics, one's responsibility for "the other" does not consider anything about "the other" except his or her "otherness." An act of mercy is not so radical. It considers context. Mercy is one thing for a pauper. It is another thing for a king. The sort of post-modern ethics described above cannot make such a rational decision. The absolute status of "the other" rejects such intellectual reflection. The other is absolute even if the other happens to be Adolph Hitler or Joseph Stalin.

Both post-modern ethics and the sort of ethical construction being attempted here are in response to the situation set in motion by the agricultural revolution. Morality emerged when food became a commodity. It was a consequence of the need for criteria to establish a person's worthiness to receive food. Both the ethics of Jesus and post-modernism are responses to the death-dealing character of morality. The difference between them is that ethics in the spirit of Jesus is grounded in alternative communities in which mercy and grace happen. Post-modern ethics is not communally based. It remains purely and unequivocally individualistic. There is "the other" in his or her isolation and there is the ethical actor in his or her isolation. Thus, post-modernism maintains the most fundamental defect of modernism, namely, its emphasis on individuality. Both modernists and post-modernists assume that each person is an isolated or cut off individual. Post-moderns try to remedy this isolation by making "the other" most fundamental, but it is still one isolated individual treating another isolated person as absolute for no reason whatsoever. The title of Enrique Dussell's book *Ethics and Community* states an alternative. Here the community and not "the other" is the starting point of ethical reflection. Many American Indian tribes knew of the primacy of community as well.

Ethics and American Indian Tribes

North American Indian tribes lived in accord with partnership ways. They did so before they encountered the European version of the dominator system.[31] In this way they are different from Euro-American Christians who have been subject to the dominator system for centuries. Developing ways to resist the dominator system is the goal of those under the spell of the dominator system. North American Indians, however, are more positive in their approach. They try to make their behavior and social organization conform to nature. Since nature differs from place to place, their behavior and organization may differ somewhat, but wherever they developed their culture, their goal was to recognize that they are in partnership with all living things.

> The task of the tribal religion, if such religion can be said to have a task, is to determine the proper relationship that the people of the tribe must have with other living things and to develop the self-discipline within the tribal community so that man acts harmoniously with other creatures. The world that he experiences is dominated by the presence of power, the manifestation of life energies, the whole life-flow of a creation. Recognition that the human being holds an important place in such a creation is tempered by the thought that they are dependent on everything in creation for their existence.[32]

We who are bewitched by civilization and its universal system of domination have tremendous difficulty understanding nature and other human beings in ways other than domination. For us nature is not to be lived-in. It is to be dominated. We have no other way to think about it. Indeed, we call anyone who thinks otherwise "uncivilized" or "idealistic," but the fact of the matter is our way is not the only way. It is not even a life affirming way. It is increasingly becoming apparent that our way is a way of death. Civilized people refuse to entertain the notion that other ways of life are possible. Accordingly, it is almost impossible for us to recognize alternatives. American Indians give us some guidance, but we must develop our own alternatives so that we do not steal their spirit like we stole their land.[33]

The words American Indians choose to share are very important because many North American Indians were not subject to the dominator system and civilization until 1492. From 1492 until the present moment, they have fought the dominator system in some way. In general, Euro-Americans think the American Indian struggle is an irrational fight against civilization and Christianity –

two supremely good things in our view. The American Indian struggle against the dominator system, however, is not irrational. It just serves values other than that of the dominator system and civilization. It is a struggle in the service of life.

In the preface to his wonderful book, *Spirit and Resistance*, George Tinker quotes a remarkable representative of the Osage tribe named *a-ki-da tonka*. He spoke these words after visiting Washington D.C. in 1822 as part of an Osage delegation.

> I see and admire your manner of living, your good warm houses, your extensive corn-fields, your gardens, your cows, oxen, workhorses, wagons and a thousand machines that I know not the use of; I see that you are able to clothe yourselves, even from weeds and grass. In short, you can do almost what you choose. You whites possess the power of (subduing) almost every animal (to your) use. You are surrounded by slaves. Everything about you is in chains, and you are slaves yourselves. I fear if I should exchange my pursuits for yours, I too should become a slave. Talk to my sons; perhaps they may be persuaded to adopt your fashions, or at least to recommend them to their sons; but for myself, I was born free, was raised free, and wish to die free. . . . I am perfectly content with my condition.[34]

This quotation shows the values of civilization were hardly universal and that other values exist that are life-affirming rather than death-dealing. Many American Indian tribes clearly understood the bondage inherent in Euro-American civilization because they lived differently. Unlike the Euro-Americans who had been born into the dominator system and indoctrinated into its ways, American Indians could see alternatives. They actually lived and continue to live these alternatives.

The difference between Indian partnership ways and our resistance to the dominator system is that our resistance must begin with repentance. The civilized ones need to turn away from morality and the dominator system in order to even see an alternative. Otherwise, we can do nothing other than what we have done. Indians do not need to repent of civilization's negative features. They did not promote them. They did not use civilization for their advantage. They are, in fact, *victims* of the death-dealing aspects of civilization. Indians do not need to repent. They need to remember. This is not my suggestion. In the words of Noble Red Man (Matthew King) an Oglala Lakota elder, "Only one thing's sadder than remembering you were once free, and that's forgetting that you were once free. That would be the saddest thing of all. That's one thing we Indians will never do."[35]

American Indian ways of life are fundamentally different from the civilized ways of the dominator system. Intuitively and/or consciously, they live in accord with nature. Nature is not to be exploited. Only after contact with civilized ones did some American Indians change their understanding of nature and their place in it.

> We did not think of the great open plains, the beautiful rolling hills, and winding streams with tangled growth as 'wild.' Only to the white men was nature a 'wilderness' and only to him was the land 'infested' with 'wild' animals and 'savage' people. To us it was tame. Earth was bountiful and we were surrounded with the blessings of the Great Mystery. Not until the hairy man from the east came and with brutal frenzy heaped injustices upon us and the families that we loved was it 'wild' for us. When the very animals of the forest began fleeing from his approach, then it was that for us the 'Wild West' began.[36]

Many Indians tribes were pre-agricultural revolution because they had not yet commoditized food. Food had yet to be placed "under lock and key." As a consequence, they were not civilized. They had not succumbed to the dominator system, and morality – with its devastating effects – had no place in their culture. Only in their encounter with the Euro-American version of the dominator system did they experience first-hand the death-dealing tactics of morality. While they may have much to teach us, we have little of value for them except our repentance. Their teaching comes through stories they choose to share. It would be nice if we listened.

George Tinker tells an illuminating story in this regard. He remembers reading a letter by General William T. Sherman on his retirement from fighting the Plains Indians. Sherman wrote that it would take much more time than anticipated to civilize the Indians because the Indians "know no greed, and, until they understand greed they will never understand the private ownership of property."[37] Not only does this comment show the fundamental status of covetousness and greed in the American version of the dominator system, but, in Tinker's view, it reveals a lack of understanding of Indian culture. "I would argue to the contrary that Indian people certainly did understand the human emotions and motivations of greed, but had powerful and complex social mechanisms for systematically suppressing them in the interest of a communal sense of wholeness and well-being."[38] American Indian tribes used ritual and story to combat covetousness and greed. Greed and covetousness are integral to the American way of life. The Indians were quite aware of these "sins." Their stories fought them.

For example, a Blackfoot story tells how the Creator gave four brothers tobacco to share with the people. It was given in order to empower the prayers of the people and help them achieve clarity of vision. The four brothers, however, kept the gift for themselves and horded its power. A married couple saw the injustice in this and set out to get tobacco for themselves. They discovered its seeds and received knowledge of how to plant tobacco as well as the rituals involved in the planting. (Rituals regarding tobacco planting were then told in the story in order to pass on this knowledge of the next generation who listened to the story). The couple planted the tobacco. It grew to maturity in four days. Just as they were about to harvest their tobacco, a hail storm destroyed the crop of the four brothers. The brothers are wiped out because they did not save some tobacco seeds. They ran to the couple and offered to make them partners and continue the process of hording the tobacco, but it was too late. The tobacco and seeds were already distributed to all the people. The social harmony the four brothers destroyed by their greed was restored.[39]

Many, many American Indian stories deny individualism and uphold the community. They are a glaring contrast to the individualism that plagues Christianity and Western philosophy both in its modern and post-modern guise. The constant telling and retelling of such stories, combined with rituals used in support of these stories emphasized community values and promoted partnership ways.

Civilized Americans have their own myths, legends and stories that similarly promote the values of American civilization. We have a myriad of sagas like George Lucas' *Star Wars* or Tolkien's *Lord of the Rings*. These promote the myth that we are engaged in a cosmological struggle between good and evil. Like Luke Skywalker or Frodo, we are the "good guys" who must kill the "bad guys" in order that good might triumph over evil.

Walter Wink has brilliantly shown that many of the cartoons our children watch and the movies we see tell a story he calls the myth of redemptive violence. He uses *Popeye* cartoons as an archetype. All *Popeye* cartoons begin with Popeye courting the alluring Olive Oyle. A violent man Bluto (in the older cartoons) or Brutus (in the newer versions) violates the peaceful tranquility. He beats Popeye to a pulp and tries a cartoon version of a sexual assault on Olive Oyle. After getting beaten within inches of death, Popeye eats spinach. This gives him god-like strength with which he destroys Bluto, saves Olive Oyle and restores the original tranquility. All is well with the world. Violence has restored the peace - at least until the next *Popeye* cartoon in which the same pattern occurs once again.[40]

The myth of redemptive violence is not limited to cartoons. Our movies repeat this myth time and time again. Clint Eastwood, Charles Bronson, Bruce Willis, Stephen Segal or Governor Schwartzenegger experience unspeakable acts of violence at the beginning of their films. The initial violent act apparently justifies the hero's even more violent response. The hero kills almost every bad guy in the film until the ultimate showdown between the hero and the arch villain occurs. The hero wins. Harmony is restored. Violence is the means of harmony's restoration.

What we *should* learn from these films and cartoons and what we actually learn are vastly different. We actually learn that violence is the answer to most problems and that it will cleanse and restore us to some utopian, pristine state. What we *should* learn from these cartoons and films is that there is always a sequel. Violence does not restore a pristine state. No one ever learns anything in a *Popeye* cartoon. Popeye never learns to eat spinach when he sees Bluto coming. Bluto never learns to moderate his behavior. Olive Oyle never gets out of these two dysfunctional relationships.[41] There is a *Death Wish* I, II and III. There is a *Rambo* I, II and III. There is a *Diehard* I, II and III. No one learns that violence has little if any cleansing power. We fail to understand that violence begets violence.

If the myth of redemptive violence were only in our cartoons and movies it would be one thing, but it influences our foreign policy as well. Woodrow Wilson called World War I (this war also had a sequel) "The war to end wars." That war was supposed to stop violence and restore tranquility. In our war on terror the response to the initial act of violence – horrible as the terrorist act was – was the same as we see in the movies. In retaliation for that despicable act, we have probably killed fifty times the innocent people that were killed on September 11, 2001. The difference between our actual response and the response of our film heroes is our films always culminate with some form of showdown between the hero and the villain. Our struggle against terrorism is unlikely to end in man to man combat between our President and Osama bin Laden.

One of the tasks of those who have "materially benefited" from the dominator system is to repent of these sorts of stories and find other stories that, like the stories of American Indians, enrich communal life. This does not mean that we adopt American Indian stories as our own. It means that we need to remember our own stories. We have already discussed a number of such stories. Most prominent among them is the Garden of Eden story. In a way, this inquiry into the relationship between ethics and morality is a continuation of this ancient story. We will now continue to interpret this ancient story with a discussion of the difference between ethical virtues and moral virtues. This is a discussion of how we who are in the grip of the dominator system might continue to repent and experience life anew.

Chapter 6:

Ethical Virtues and Tactics

> "Tell me, you who are kind enough to listen, what becomes of my smile when I stop smiling?"

Elie Wiesel[1]

Morality and ethics serve different worldviews. Morality serves civilization and the dominator system. It draws the divide between good and evil. It separates the good and worthy from the evil and unworthy. We have seen that the moral criteria used to distinguish between good and evil differ from civilization to civilization. We have also seen that the social function of morality is the same in all civilizations. Morality marginalizes those it deems evil. It leaves the evil ones for dead, and it justifies the moral people when they marginalize those deemed immoral. In contrast, ethics recognizes that the distinctions made between good and evil are of human origin and design. Ethics serves life by identifying with people and other life forms that morality has marginalized and left for dead. Morality and ethics serve different masters. Accordingly, moral actions and attitudes usually differ from ethical actions and attitudes. This chapter describes this contrast.

In his book *After Virtue*, Alasdair MacIntrye describes a *virtue* as an attitude or activity that enables a person to receive goods internal to a practice.[2] A practice is a commonly agreed upon activity that has standards, rules, a history and certain authorities. MacIntyre says games, like chess and baseball, arts, like music and painting, and professions, like medicine and law, are examples of practices. Each practice has two sorts of "goods." There are goods internal to the practice and goods external to the practice. Money, power and prestige are examples of goods external to a practice. They are external because they are awarded by those outside the practice to those inside the practice. The adulation of the fans is an external good to the practice of basketball, hockey, baseball, football and soccer. The money athletes receive is also a good external to the practice. Goods internal to the practice are different. They are derived from the performance of the practice itself. In other words, those who have mastered particular practices would find a way to perform such practices regardless of external reward. *Virtues are activities and actions that are necessary to receive goods internal to a practice.*[3]

Science is a good example of a practice because it has standards, history and authorities. The goods internal to the practice of science are associated with participation within the scientific community and with the joy of scientific work itself. Honesty, courage and justice are three scientific virtues because they are activities and actions necessary to receive goods internal to the practice of science. Scientific courage does not involve facing enemy guns, but in the context of the scientific community courage can be described – as Aristotle would describe any act of courage – as the mean between rashness and cowardliness. The scientific community would cease to exist if scientists lacked the courage to publish because new ideas necessary for the growth and enrichment of the scientific community would not be exchanged. On the other hand, scientific community would be undermined if its members published rashly. If anything whatsoever was published or presented at a meeting of scientists, the community would be deluged with material. There would be so much material that the community would not be able to distinguish between good science and bad science. The scientific community's life is enhanced by courage - the mean between rashness and cowardliness. Courage limits the number of publications and gives the community new information to discuss and critique. In this way, courage gives life to the scientific community, and scientists can receive goods internal to the practice of science.

By the same token, scientists tolerate a great deal of bad science. What they cannot tolerate is dishonesty because dishonesty undermines the integrity of the scientific community. Scientists must be able to trust the work of other scientists. The scientific enterprise would crumble if scientists could not rely on the honesty of other scientists because individual scientists would always have to "reinvent the wheel." Since honesty supports the scientific community, and since it is through the community that scientists receive goods internal to the practice of science, honesty is also a scientific virtue because it is an attitude or activity that enables a scientist to receive goods internal to the practice of science.

MacIntyre readily declares that the virtues in one practice may not be consistent with the virtues in another.[4] Virtues of a warrior are not the same as the virtues associated with the practice of farming. The virtues of ancient Greek culture are different from the virtues of modern Germany. This is also the case with the dominator system and partnership ways. The dominator system is engaged in the practice of civilization. It has virtues that are consistent with this practice. Partnership ways are engaged in the practice of life. They have virtues that are consistent with life. The virtues of the dominator system differ from the virtues associated with partnership because different attitudes and actions are necessary to achieve goods internal to these different practices. The virtues of the dominator system include: morality, ranking and hierarchy building, unilateral power, one dimensional communication, justification, mastery and vengeance. The virtues of partnership include: ethics, community building, communal power, listening, confession, humility and forgiveness (see Appendix). It is beyond dispute that the virtues consistent with the dominator model have allowed those who practice them to achieve goods internal to the practice of domination, but our constant wars, poverty and looming ecological crisis may indicate that the practice of domination may no longer be sustainable. Different virtues need to be practiced in order to support the life affirming activities of partnership. We will now contrast some of the virtues of partnership with those of the dominator system.

Communal Power

Unilateral power is the only sort of power the dominator system employs. Indeed, those under the spell of the dominator system cannot conceive of power in any other way. Unilateral power is "the capacity to influence, guide, adjust, manipulate, shape, control or transform the human and natural environment in order to advance one's own purposes."[5] Unilateral power involves moving and influencing others without being subject to the influence of others. Accordingly, inequality and ranking – the most fundamental characteristics of the dominator system – are two of unilateral power's essential features. Concerns about status, station and rank have always been central to those who exercise unilateral power. Since civilized people have difficulty distinguishing between their lives and their status, those who possess unilateral power seldom relinquish it voluntarily. Doing so is synonymous with abandoning one's rank and social status. The powerful seldom make voluntary concessions to the powerless. Concessions are forced only when rivals gain enough unilateral power to force them. Throughout American history, agents of social change - labor unions, advocates for women's rights and civil rights groups - first developed a power base. Only then could they force concessions.[6] The history of the dominator system shows that people with unilateral power will only listen if those who speak have enough political clout to force them to do so.

There is an important corollary to this observation. Those who possess unilateral power are indifferent to those who do not have unilateral power. The powerless can be ignored. They are easily marginalized.[7] Unilateral power can ignore the poor who are silenced by the weight of their poverty. It ignores generations yet to be born as it tries to wrest the last bit of treasure from the earth. Even the most "liberal" democracies ignore the voiceless ones.

Unilateral power is death-dealing. It is a power only because of its ability to kill. As noted, unilateral power is the ability to move others without oneself being moved. Such manipulation needs a world of objects because objects do not rebel. Objects do not have minds of their own. When beings actually have minds of their own, they often challenge unilateral power. Thus unilateral power works best when the external world is composed of objects or of living beings willing to be treated as objects. Unilateral power's relationship to death becomes apparent the moment one understands that a living thing dies the moment it becomes just an object.

Unilateral power does not always in fact kill. It does not always need to be so extreme. It can force us to cooperate. We cooperate by acting as if we are dead. Most of us prefer this metaphorical death to the real thing, so we cooperate with the dictates of unilateral power. We cooperate by acting like objects. Generally the poor and the marginalized act like objects because of the unadulterated threat of death or imprisonment. We who morality declares good and acceptable cooperate because we think we benefit from such cooperation. In MacIntyre's words, we receive goods internal to the practice of civilization when we use or subject ourselves to unilateral power. We are, in fact, compensated for such cooperation. We receive living wages, retirement plans, praise, prestige and sometimes even health care. We mistakenly believe our lives depend on these benefits, so we cooperate with unilateral power and death.

Certain employer/employee relationships are illustrative of such cooperation. It is not unusual for employees to obey a memo demanding their presence at a meeting. It is also not unusual for the meeting to be a total waste of employees' time, yet the meeting is attended nonetheless. In such situations, employees turn themselves into objects. They move their bodies into the meeting room like furniture movers might move tables and chairs. They do so because of the benefits that civilization, morality and the dominator system bestow on those deemed good and acceptable. Rarely do we understand that when we act like this, we are acting as if we are dead. As previously stated, we prefer a metaphorical death to the real thing.

Jesus rejected unilateral power because of its association with death. In Mark 10: 35-45 Jesus' disciples James and John ask Jesus if they can sit one at his right hand and one at his left when Jesus comes to his glory. Surprisingly, Jesus says that such a request is beyond his power to grant. Then he turned and said to all his disciples:

> You know that those who are supposed to rule over the Gentiles lord it over them, and their great men exercise authority over them. But it shall not be so among you; but whoever would be great among you must be your servant and whoever would be first among you must be slave of all. For the Son of Man came not to be served but to serve, and to give his life as a ransom for many. (Mk 10: 41-45).

Jesus always rejected unilateral power. He refused to use it even though this refusal probably cost him his life. On the night he was betrayed, he told his followers to put away their swords and not defend him. He refused to defend himself before Pilate. He did not answer any of his questions. He forgave his executioners. He rejected unilateral power to the end.

Saying Jesus rejected unilateral power is not the same as saying that Jesus was powerless because unilateral power is not the only kind of power there is. It is just the only kind of power the dominator system uses. Jesus used a different kind of power. The power Jesus employed receives its authority from life instead of death. Peter Paris calls this sort of power communal power, and communal power is a virtue of partnership ways. *Communal power is the capacity to influence others while being influenced by others.* It is a power that recognizes the primacy of community to promote and enrich the world.[8] Communal power is not passive. It is a power that resides in the community's capacity to change itself, its members and the world at large.[9] The American Civil Rights movement is an important example of how communal power functions.

> C. Eric Lincoln argues that the decisive difference between the Montgomery bus boycott and the history of black churches (to that point in history) is that the black religious leaders for the first time challenged the white establishment over something specific, in which one side or the other had to emerge as victor. The victory that blacks achieved in that event was unprecedented, and it changed the whole history of the black struggle for racial justice to say nothing of the psychological impact on all who participated directly or indi-

rectly. That type of activity enabled blacks to become initiators of action rather than respondents.
*In that event, we see black religious leaders utiliz-
ing communal power in its full sense, that is, aim-
ing at producing an effect and undergoing an
effect both in the interest of enhancing community.*[10]

The civil rights movement shows communal power is not
passive. It might be described as non-violent, but it is not passive.
It produces an effect. It also demonstrates the difference between
communal power and unilateral power. Unilateral power moves in
one direction. It moves outward from an unmoved center against a
world of objects. Communal power produces an effect on others,
but those using it undergo an effect as well. Communal power
changes those who use it as well as those it seeks to change. In the
case of the civil rights movement, the black community underwent
many effects. They were beaten, killed and intimidated. They also
made great strides in gaining their civil rights. Indeed, they
probably would not have gained their rights if they had not been
willing to undergo an effect. The power to risk themselves in the
struggle stemmed from their churches and their communities. The
participants in the struggle transformed the society at large and
were transformed by the society at large. The use of communal
power creates and enhances community because it cannot be
employed without others. Benefits are bestowed through such
diversity.

Listening

Those in the grip of the dominator system are much more
concerned with being understood than they are with understanding
someone else. Hierarchy demands this. The rules of hierarchy are
such that your boss does not need to understand you. You need to
understand your boss. In a patriarchal family, the father does not
need to understand his wife or children. His wife and children
need to understand him. In the military, the general does not
consult the private. The private takes orders from the general.
Clearly hierarchy demands communication, but it is one-way
communication. It originates at the summit of the hierarchy, and it

seeks to influence those of lower degree without being influenced from below.

Communication is the expedient transmission of information within the dominator system. Information moves from a center to a periphery or from top to bottom. In other words, communication follows the path blazed by unilateral power. Partnership, on the other hand, strives for conversation. Conversation follows the path of communal power whereby all parties to the conversation move others while being moved themselves. Conversation requires the commitment to listen to the other. Conversation does not happen if listening does not occur. Listening, therefore, is a partnership virtue through which a person gains goods internal to the practice of partnership.

Listening does not simply involve understanding a particular communication. It is not even the ability to repeat exactly what has been said. It might not even be related to doing what the one speaking has proposed. These traits are more involved with the reception of a communication than they are with listening. *Listening involves making an adjustment in one's life on the basis of what is heard.* Those under the spell of the dominator system think listening entails agreement or doing what was proposed. Parents who understand listening in this way often say that their child did not listen to them when the child did not do that which the parents proposed. In fact, a child can listen to his or her parents and not do what was suggested. An adjustment can be made in the child's life on the basis of what was said even though the parental suggestions were not followed. It is, however, important for the listening party to state how he or she is making an adjustment on the basis of what was heard. Such a response reinforces the relationship between the parties to the conversation and enriches the life of the relationship. This is just one small example of how listening is a virtue through which people receive goods internal to the practice of life.

The Gospel of Matthew demonstrates the communal importance of listening in the following account of an excommunication. An excommunication is an excellent place to see what is vital to a community because the values of a group are revealed when someone is forced to leave.

If your brother sins against you, go and tell him his fault between you and him alone. *If he listens to you,* you have gained a brother. But if *he does not listen,* take one or two others along with you, that every word may be confirmed by the evidence of two or three witnesses. *If he refuses to listen to them,* tell it to the church, and *if he refuses to listen even to the church,* let him be to you as a Gentile or tax collector. (Mt. 18: 15-18)

The brother is not expelled because of the original sin. He is dismissed because he did not listen! He did not listen to the one against whom the alleged sin was committed. He refused to listen when two others heard the complaint, and finally, he did not listen to the church. The passage never mentions the nature of the initial sin or grievance. The refusal to listen is what is important.

If listening is making an adjustment in one's life on the basis of information that has been received, then the brother who refused to listen did not make such an adjustment. The brother either acted as though the complaint had no merit or as if the complaint was never made. In refusing to listen, the brother treated the one complaining, the two witnesses and the entire congregation as if what they said made absolutely no difference in his life. He treated them as if they did not exist. He treated them as if they were dead or as if they were objects to be ignored.

Listening is uncivilized activity. This is evident the moment one asks, "Who is more likely not to listen?" On a superficial level, the one who is more likely not to listen is the one who does not want to change or make an adjustment. This leads to a more profound contention. The one who does not want to make an adjustment is usually the one with the most to lose. Included in this group are the rich, powerful, religious and educated – the people normally of high rank in dominator cultures. For example, since it is difficult to change an educated person's mind about the things in which he or she is most educated, an educated person is less likely to listen. A person with a Ph.D. in theology is unlikely to change his or her mind about a doctrinal matter if challenged by a lay person. This is not to say that the challenge cannot be correct or insightful. It is just to say that a person with a Ph.D. has devoted too much time and effort to change his or her educated judgment based upon an uneducated person's insight. It is not impossible. It is just very unlikely. These same comments apply to the powerful and the rich. Adjustments place riches and power at risk; hence, the rich and powerful are less likely to listen. It is not that it is impossible for them to listen. It is just unlikely. They have too much to protect. By the same token, the powerless, the poor and the uneducated are probably more likely to make the adjustments required in order to listen. Once again, this does not guarantee they will listen. They are just more likely to listen than the educated, the politically powerful and the rich.

The Church has always had its share of rich, powerful, educated people. Consequently, its history is replete with instances in which its leaders refuse to listen. Instead of listening, they protect their position, power, riches, doctrine and prestige. This means that it is more likely that the excommunicated one in Matthew's text was a rich, powerful, educated leader than a neophyte follower of Jesus.

Perhaps the reason that Matthew's community thought it ought to be a listening community is that they believed their community ought to reflect the fact that their God listens. Specifically God listens to prayer. The gods of the dominator system do not listen to prayers. In the dominator system, prayers and sacrifice are indeed required to placate the deity. Prayers and ritual regulate the behavior of the people, but prayers cannot change a deity's mind. The gods of the dominator system do not listen. Like Aristotle's unmoved mover, the gods of the dominator system sit at the apex of the hierarchical order. They remain unmoved by whatever is beneath them. It is a waste of time to pray to such gods because they do not listen. To be sure, the gods of the dominator system communicate. They make their demands, but they do not make adjustments. The Biblical God, however, often makes an adjustment on the basis of what has been communicated.

This conflict, between the Biblical God who listens and the dominator God who remains unmoved, can be seen in an interesting textual change that occurred in a familiar story from the Old Testament. In Genesis 18, God has come down to see for himself if the reports he has heard about Sodom and Gomorrah are true. In Genesis 18: 17, God wonders if he should hide this agenda from Abraham, but chooses otherwise and informs Abraham of his mission and intent. The text that we now have says, "So the men turned from there and went toward Sodom, while *Abraham remained standing before the Lord."* (Gen. 18: 22).

> We may observe a remarkable textual problem that illuminates (this) matter. As it stands, the text in 18: 22 now says, "Abraham stood before the Lord," suggesting the subordination of Abraham to Yahweh. This is what we should expect. But a very early text – not to be doubted in its authority and authenticity – shows that the text before any translation originally said, "Yahweh stood before Abraham." . . . It is as though Abraham was presiding over the meeting. But the bold image of Yahweh being accountable to Abraham for this theological idea was judged by the scribes as irreverent and unacceptable.[11]

The text as originally written – with Yahweh standing before Abraham – probably was deemed "irreverent and unacceptable" because it violated the dominator system's understanding of God. According to such an understanding, God cannot be influenced by beings of lower rank. As long as these scribes were under the influence of the dominator system, they could not even begin to understand what was right in front of their eyes. They could not believe God makes adjustments. They could not believe God listens so they changed the text to read, "Abraham remained standing before God."

The adjustment God made is reflected in the question Abraham asks God. "Will you sweep away the righteous with the wicked? Suppose there are fifty righteous within the city; will you not sweep away the place and forgive it for the sake of the fifty righteous who are in it. *Far be it from you to do such a thing, to slay the righteous with the wicked."* (Gen. 18: 23-25). Those who know this story will remember that eventually Abraham got God to agree that Sodom would not be destroyed for the sake of ten righteous people. Unfortunately, ten were not found, and the place was destroyed. A cynic might argue that God allowed Abraham to argue down to ten righteous people because God knew in advance that there were not that many righteous people in the city. This interpretation actually makes sense from an ideological perspective that assumes that God knows all facts in detail.

This ideological perspective, however, is not consistent with the text. Genesis 18: 20, 21 indicates that God is on a fact finding mission. "I must go down and see whether they have done altogether according to the outcry that has come to me; and if not, I will know." (Gen 18:21). Fidelity to the text, therefore, indicates that God does not know if ten righteous people exist in Sodom and Gomorrah. Thus it can be said that in this instance Abraham is God's theological mentor.[12] Abraham is *teaching* God that the righteous should not be killed with the unrighteous! Just as being chosen by God is new to Abraham, what it means to have chosen Abraham is new to God. For this relationship to work, God must listen. God must make an adjustment on the basis of information Abraham provided.

This story is not unique. At another crucial point in the history of Israel, Israel's survival depends on God listening. In Exodus 32: 7-14, the people of Israel have been emancipated from their Egyptian captivity, and Moses is about to receive the Ten Commandments on Mt. Sinai. Much time passes. The Israelites grow impatient. They wonder if Moses is alive. They demand that Aaron make them a god to lead them, and Aaron complies. He gathers jewelry from the people and quickly fashions a golden bull. He tells Israel that this is their God. Seeing this from Mt. Sinai, Yahweh gets angry!! The following conversation with Moses ensues.

> And the Lord said to Moses, "Go down; for *your* people whom *you* brought up out of the land of Egypt have corrupted themselves. They have turned aside quickly out of the way which I commanded them; they have made for themselves a molten calf, and have worshipped it and sacrificed to it and said, 'These are your gods O' Israel, who brought you up out of the land of Egypt.'" And the Lord said to Moses, "I have seen this people, and behold, it is a stiff-necked people; now therefore let me alone, that my wrath may burn hot against them and I may consume them; but of you I will make a great nation."
>
> But Moses besought the Lord his God and said, "O Lord, why does *your* wrath burn hot against *your* people, whom *you* have brought from out of

Egypt with great power and a mighty hand? Why should the Egyptians say, 'With evil intent did he bring them forth to slay them in the mountains, and to consume them from the face of the earth?' Turn from your fierce wrath and *repent of the evil* against your people. Remember Abraham, Isaac and Israel, your servants to whom you swore by your own self, and said to them, "I will multiply your descendants as stars of heaven, and all this land I have possessed I will give to your descendants and they shall inherit it forever." *And the Lord repented of the evil* which he thought to do to his people. (Ex. 32: 7-14).

According to Brevard Childs, the key moment in this passage happens when Moses *disobeys* God. God told Moses to leave him alone so his wrath can be executed against Israel. Moses did not comply.[13] Had the Biblical God been like the gods of the dominator system, Moses would have had no alternative but to comply. Such gods do not listen. Such gods do not make adjustments. Clearly such gods do not repent. The surprise is that Moses does not obey God. He does not leave God alone. He challenges God's intentions. Childs notes that Moses makes three points in his subsequent conversation (prayer) with God. First, Moses suggests that the newly emancipated slaves are pretty new at being God's chosen people. Accordingly, God should make allowances. Second, Moses tells God it would be bad public relations if God killed the Israelites in the desert. The Egyptians would never let God hear the end of it. Finally, Moses tells God to remember the promises made to Abraham, Isaac and Jacob. This persuades God to *"repent of the evil he was about to do to Israel."*[14]

This extraordinary story is essential to the entire Biblical narrative because there would have been no story at all if God had not listened to Moses and repented. Israel owes its life to the fact that its God is one who listens and makes adjustments on the basis of what was heard. Faithful communities reflect these characteristics. Such communities are listening communities. They listen to their God and to each other. They would be even more consistent if they also listened to the plants, animals and the rest of nature as do many cultures the Western world has classified as uncivilized.

Humility

Humility is closely related to other ethical virtues. A humble person would be likely to listen to others and make adjustments. A humble person would be more likely to acknowledge and confess a sin or mistake. A humble person would be less likely to impose his or her will by using unilateral power.

The dominator system has no use for humility. It strives for mastery instead.[15] Civilized ones try to be masters of what they survey. They are to be the master of nature (an unlikely prospect if one were to reflect upon this goal for five minutes). They put all things under their feet. They control as many people as possible. They issue orders. They move others without being moved. They avoid being influenced by others. Mastery is the virtue of the dominator system. Life, however, can no longer afford the arrogance that is the consequence of our quest for mastery. Life would benefit greatly by humility. Were we a little more humble, countless wars would have been avoided and environmental disasters might be less common. Humility is a virtue of partnership ways because humility is an activity or attitude that allows us to receive goods internal to the practice of life.

Humility is a more realistic virtue than is mastery because, as the joke goes, we have much to be humble about. For example, humility recognizes that there are always some unknown consequences to any action. These unknown consequences are often inadvertent. For example, in pursuit of profit a corporation once deemed it necessary to build a road from point A to point B. The corporation's intent was to make transportation easier and more profitable. The workers who built the road, however, were infected by a virus found in an animal indigenous to the area. This virus had not had the opportunity to spread to human beings because the animal had only limited contact with human beings prior to the road's construction. Unfortunately, the infected workers spread the virus into the human population. The inadvertent consequences were deadly. This is not a hypothetical scenario. Something like this happened during the construction of the Belem-Brasilia highway in the 1960s. According to The Harvard Working Group on New and Resurgent Diseases, contact with a sloth indigenous to the region the road traversed gave the workers the Oropouche virus which was spread to the human population.[16] Clearly the people had no intention of starting an epidemic. This was an unintended consequence.

Unintended consequences are not limited to the transmission of disease. Nearly every technology has unintended consequences. It is the contention of this essay, for example, that morality itself is an unintended consequence of the agricultural revolution's commoditization of food. The automobile had the unintended consequences of air pollution, the death of 30,000 Americans a year and a mammoth network of concrete roads that has destroyed some communities and created some unintended ecological problems.

Humility makes us slow down and actually think about what the unintended consequences of an action or an invention might be. Remembering the fact that there are usually unintended consequences makes it more likely rather than less likely we will be able to deal with unintended consequences when they arise. Arrogance and mastery make it less likely for us to admit an unintended consequence occurred. Arrogance and mastery lead us to "stay the course" even when the terrible ramifications of an act are apparent to nearly everyone. The masters find it difficult to hear about unintended consequences because unintended consequences indicate the lack of mastery. Rather than admit that one is not the master, we continue to follow paths that lead to death and destruction. The greatest danger to human survival may be our arrogance, and our arrogance is a consequence of the dominator model's need of mastery. Humility is not a threat to life. Mastery is.

The virtue called humility demands we recognize that all our decisions and actions happen in the context of some ignorance. Humility makes us stop and reflect on the actions we propose. This is far more difficult than it sounds, for our modern technological culture does not allow us to stop and reflect. Nonetheless, we need more of this Socratic humility. Legend says the Oracle at Delphi told Socrates that he was wisest of all people. Socrates thought the Oracle wrong because Socrates knew he did not know anything. To prove the Oracle wrong, Socrates proceeded to interview everyone who claimed to have knowledge. These discussions revealed two things to Socrates. First, those who claimed knowledge really did not have the knowledge they claimed. Second, the Oracle was correct about the wisdom of Socrates. Socrates knew he did not know. Others thought they knew something when, in fact, they knew nothing. In knowing he did not know Socrates knew more than everyone else. The Oracle was correct. Socrates was the wisest of all Athenians because of his humility.

The practice of humility supports and enriches life on the individual, communal, national and even the geo-political level. For example, it has often been argued that the Treaty of Versailles which ended World War I was quite vindictive to the Germans. It cast the Germans as solely responsible of the war, and it demanded reparations that were extremely burdensome on the Germans. It is often theorized that had the peace treaty been less severe, democracy might have succeeded in Germany. The Nazis might not have come to power, and World War II might have been avoided. Those who agree with this popular assessment of the Treaty of Versailles imply that the reason for the German post-war plight is the arrogance of the allies in imposing the treaty on the Germans. Had they acted with some humility, they might have acknowledged the fact that the Germans were not solely responsible for the war. Had the allies humbly acknowledged some responsibility for they war, they might have reduced the burden they placed on the Germans. Absent such a burden, German democracy might have survived, rampant inflation might have been avoided. Hitler might not have come to power. World War II might have been avoided. The Holocaust could have been prevented. The current turmoil in the Middle East would be different and nuclear weapons may never have been invented. In short, we would live in a decidedly different world if humility instead of arrogance had been the virtue employed by the allies at Versailles. This world would still have its problems, but the problems we might be facing might not be as much of a threat to human existence as they now are.

Our lack of humility has global consequences. Nearly every tragic event in human history would have been moderated considerably if the parties engaged had practiced a little humility. Humility, however, is an unusual character trait of leaders in the dominator system. The system values the illusion of mastery. Arrogance, rather than humility, is always associated with this illusion.

Forgiveness and Mercy

The dominator system bestows rights on those it deems worthy. In other words, those who find themselves on the proper side of the moral divide have certain rights. Those who fall on the evil side of the moral divide find their rights limited or eliminated. Nazi Germany conferred rights on Aryans. It denied even the right to exist to Jews and Gypsies. The *Declaration of Independence* stated that *all men* have certain inalienable rights, and the U.S. constitution subsequently denied these rights to American Indians, African slaves and women. Today there is some question about whether or not rights should extend to gay and lesbian people. Under the dominator system, the issue is always rights. The civil rights movement tried to extend these rights to African Americans. The women's liberation movement desired to extend rights to women. People concerned about the welfare of gay and lesbian people want to make sure their rights are not violated on the basis of sexual preference. Anti-abortion groups want to extend the right to life to human embryos. Others argue that foreign terrorists have the right to a trial and cannot be imprisoned indefinitely.

The struggle for rights is one of the most important struggles within the dominator system because those who have rights have the right to live in the dominator system and those without rights simply do not have the right to live within the dominator system. Moreover, we who are subject to the dominator system are trained to equate a person's rights with life itself. There is reason to equate the two. If a person has no rights, that person lacks the protection of the law and risks death. The acquisition of rights is therefore a good internal to the practice of the dominator model. One's rights give access to the benefits of civilization. Without rights, a person's very life is at risk.

Forgiveness is another virtue associated with partnership and life. It runs counter to the dominator system because the one who forgives refuses to insist on his or her rights. Forgiveness is an act of courage for subjects of the dominator system because people who forgive act like their own rights are irrelevant. (They do *not* act like the rights of others are irrelevant). Under the dominator system, a person's rights are determined by a person's rank or position in the social order. Denying one's own rights denies one's rank and prestige. It can lead to social marginalization and sometimes death. If forgiving means refusing to insist on one's rights, then we risk marginalization and even death when we forgive. Let's be clear, practicing the virtues of partnership – forgiveness, confession, mercy, communal power, humility and listening – can get you into trouble. You could risk your life employing them because they might be seen as signs of weakness by people bewitched by the dominator system.

That being said, forgiveness is a virtue of partnership ways because acts of forgiveness bestow life. Few recognize this, but the truth of this assertion becomes obvious if we ask, "How many relationships have crumbled because of our inability to forgive?" "How many marriages die because wives cannot forgive their husbands or husbands cannot forgive their wives?" "How many wars have been fought because nations cannot forgive?" "How many murders have there been . .?" On the other hand, "How many marriages live because a spouse had the courage to forgive?" "How many children have been born because such forgiveness occurred?" "How many lives would be saved if forgiveness among nations became the norm?" The gift of life is the good internal to the practice of the partnership virtue of forgiveness.

The relationship between forgiveness and life as well as our preference for the unforgiving ways of the dominator system is illustrated in the following parable of Jesus.

> Therefore the kingdom of heaven may be compared to a king who wished to settle accounts with his servants. When he began the reckoning, one was brought to him who owed him 10,000 talents; as he could not pay, the lord ordered him to be sold, with his wife and children and all that he had, and payment be made. So the servant fell on his knees, imploring him, "Lord, have patience with me, and I will pay you everything." And out of pity for him the lord of the servant released him and forgave him the debt. But that same servant, as he went out, came upon a fellow servant who owed him one hundred denarii, and seizing him by the throat said, "Pay what you owe." So his fellow servant fell down and besought him, "Have patience with me, and I will pay you." He refused

and went and put him in prison till he should pay his debt. When his fellow servants saw what had taken place, they were greatly distressed and they went and reported to their lord what had taken place. Then his lord summoned him and said to him, "You wicked servant. I forgave you all that debt because you asked me; and should not you have mercy on your fellow servant as I had mercy on you?" And in anger his lord delivered him to the jailers, till he should pay all of his debt (Mt. 18: 23-35).

This story illustrates what has been said about forgiveness. It shows that forgiveness is refusing to insist on one's rights. No one could have condemned the lord if he had thrown the servant and his family into prison. He had the right to do so. He would have been justified in so doing. The lord, however, did not insist on his rights. He forgave his servant. This also shows forgiveness is life-giving. The lord made new life possible for his servant and his family when he forgave his servant the debt. Free from the burden of debt,* the forgiven servant could walk in newness of life. Freed from the burden of debt, the servant could have been an agent of life. He could have given the same gift of life to his fellow servant.

In the terminology of this inquiry, the lord was acting in accord with partnership ways. Partnership ways give and support life. The lord's act of forgiveness did just this. The servant, however, still wanted to live by the morality of the dominator system. He insisted on his rights. He demanded payment from his fellow servant. When his fellow servant could not pay, he threw him into jail. He had every right to do so – at least from the standpoint of the dominator system.

The forgiven servant refused partnership ways. He refused to forgive. He refused to support the life of his fellow servant. As a consequence, his lord got angry and threw him into prison. The irony is that this prison is of the unforgiving servant's own design.

---

* One denarius was a day's wage for a laborer. One talent was 6000 denarii. Thus 10,000 talents was 600 million denarii or 600 million days of labor. In other words, the forgiven one would have spent billions of life-times paying off his debt had he not been forgiven.

The lord's initial design was for the servant and his family to be sold into slavery and his property sold as well. The punishment he now receives is imprisonment until he repays his debt. This was exactly the punishment the unforgiving servant designed for the one he refused to forgive.

Furthermore, this prison of his own design is a consequence of his preference for the dominator system. Indeed, our preference for the dominator system places us in a prison of our own design. For some, this prison is pretty luxurious. So much so that we may not even recognize it to be a prison at all. For most, however, the prison is not very luxurious. It is reflected in our inability to deal with poverty, educate our young, provide decent healthcare or stop an endless war. Our inability to forgive creates prisons of our own design. This is unfortunate because all ethical virtues - forgiveness, communal power, listening, confession and humility - unlock the cells that imprison our selves and others.

Confession

Justification is a virtue of morality and the dominator system. Confession is a virtue of ethics and partnership. Under any moral scheme people must demonstrate that they belong on the "good" side of the moral divide. Such a demonstration is called justification. Since each civilization uses different criteria to establish a person or group's position on the "good" side of the moral divide, the way we justify ourselves assumes many forms. If a culture determines worth on the basis of heritage, justification involves demonstrating one's biological connection to those with the proper pedigree. If a civilization determines a person's worth on the basis of merit, justification involves doing those things that bring merit. If a particular government contends that it is always best to do the greatest good for the greatest number, justification involves making calculations that demonstrate that the greatest good has been achieved. Justification assumes many forms because different moralities demand different sorts of justification. Despite this variety, however, justification itself is universal to morality. It is the way a person or group establishes the validity of their position on the "good" side of the moral divide.

Confession, an ethical virtue, is anathema within the dominator system because the one who confesses seems to place herself on the evil side of the moral divide. This is suicide in the dominator system because, according to this worldview, the one who confesses admits she should be marginalized. It is for this reason that the powerful rarely confess. At best they say, "Mistakes were made." Rarely will the phrase, "I made a mistake" be uttered. Rarely will there be an apology. To do so within the dominator system places everything at risk.

Like humility, confession is an ethical virtue that begins with the notion of limitation. It recognizes that our thoughts and actions are always limited by our ignorance and perhaps by our sin. The dominator system understands confession differently. It believes that confession's purpose is to assuage guilt. Confession has a different purpose under partnership. It fights evil. Do not be confused by the mention of the word evil. In its refusal to draw the moral divide between good and evil, ethics does not deny the reality of evil. It merely rejects the moral belief that evil is the opposite of good. In the Hebrew Bible, for example, evil is not the opposite of good at all. Indeed, the Garden of Eden story suggests that the original sin was to understand evil as the opposite of good. It is probably more accurate to say that in Scripture the opposite of good is "not good" and evil is the opposite of life. More technically, *evil is a seemingly autonomous force that opposes life. It emerges when we do not acknowledge and confess sins, misdeeds, ignorance, errors or mistakes.* Evil opposes life. Confession is how we begin to fight evil.

Walter Brueggemann demonstrates this relationship between evil and our refusal or inability to acknowledge or confess our sins or misdeeds with a very interesting interpretation of the David and Bathsheba story.[17] The first act of this drama is quite simple. David is bored. He is walking on the roof of his palace. From this lofty vantage point, David spies the lovely Bathsheba bathing below in what she apparently thinks is the privacy of her own property. He inquires about her. He is told that she is the wife of Uriah the Hittite, one of David's most loyal and able generals. David calls for Bathsheba. He "makes love to her" (today we would call this rape, for, no one turns down the King). Bathsheba gets pregnant! (II Samuel 11: 1-5). An irretrievable act has now been committed.[18] David, who probably prided himself as being a man who could handle almost any situation, realized that he now had at least two options. First, he could acknowledge and confess the act, but this might place his throne at risk. Second, he could refuse to acknowledge his error or sin. He chose the second option, and, when such a refusal happens at high levels of government, we have what we now call a cover-up.

David sent word to his commanding general Joab asking that Joab send Uriah the Hittite to David. When Uriah arrived, David asked him how the war was going and made other small talk, and, in the end, suggested that Uriah go down to his house for the evening to "wash his feet" as the Revised Standard Version of the Bible translates the suggestion. Obviously, David figured that if he could get Uriah to make love to his wife, then David's problem would be over and things could get back to normal. Unfortunately for David's scheme, Uriah refused the offer. His loyalty to his men and to David himself prevented him from doing what the king suggested. Uriah would not take liberties that the fighting men under his command could not have while engaged in battle. Being the king, David did not plead with Uriah, but suggested that Uriah stay another day before returning to Joab. Uriah obeyed, and David threw a party that night hoping to get Uriah drunk enough so that he would visit his wife Bathsheba. It did not work. Uriah never went to see his wife. (II Samuel 11: 6-13).

David now tried another approach which, frankly, makes him a mass murderer. Rather than confess his sin to Uriah, David asked Uriah to deliver a letter to Joab. The letter ordered Joab to put Uriah in the most dangerous place in battle and then to draw back from him so the "he may be struck down and die." Joab obeyed. Uriah died. Joab sent a messenger to inform David. Upon hearing the news, David told the messenger to tell Joab, "Do not let this matter trouble you, for the sword devours now one and now another; strengthen your attack on the city, and overthrow it." (II Samuel 11: 14-25).

What began late one afternoon when David the king took advantage of Uriah's wife Bathsheba, ended in a mass murder. David, the King of Israel and Judah, the "master" of all he surveyed, was out of control. His refusal to acknowledge and confess his action unleashed the power of evil. It was not David's intention to kill his loyal general and all the men who died with him, but this consequence was a result of his failure to confess. In his failure to confess, David unleashed evil – the seemingly autonomous force in opposition to life that emerges when we refuse to acknowledge our errors, mistakes or sins. Evil's power would not have emerged if David had confessed his error, but David was unwilling to confess. Instead, David continued the cover-up. As already indicated, David advised Joab not to let this matter trouble him, or, as Walter Brueggeman has translated the passage, "Do not let this thing be *evil* in your eyes."[19] David wants Joab to chalk this up to the fortunes of war which, of course, is not the true interpretation of this event. David then marries Uriah's wife – after the proper period of mourning of course. All seems calm. It looks like the cover-up has succeeded! But then the prophet Nathan emerges. Like all prophets, Nathan speaks a truth to power which forces David to confess.

The David and Bathsheba story plays out in centers of power to this day. In each case, the refusal to acknowledge and confess one's sin, mistake or error unleashes evil – the seemingly autonomous force that opposes life. This dynamic is not limited to our power centers. On a purely personal level, if I tell a particularly unflattering lie about you, a number of things can happen. At best the lie is not repeated. Very little happens. The damage is minimal. At worst, the lie is repeated again and again. Everyone hears it. You begin to notice that people are treating you differently. You do not understand why. You ask your best friend, but she does not want to discuss it. After much provocation, however, she tells you. You, of course, deny the allegation. This does not placate her. She assumed you would not admit "the truth." People like you never do.

This example illustrates how evil emerges even on a personal level whenever sins or misdeeds are not acknowledged or confessed. My lie unleashed a power that opposes your life in the community. Since your life enriches the life of the community, the power my lie unleashed opposes the life of the community as well. It seems autonomous. It roams wherever the lie is heard. It does damage wherever it roams. It appears to be out of control. Evil's power, however, only seems to be autonomous. (Remember evil here defined is a *seemingly* autonomous force that opposes life). The actual source of this life threatening power, however, is my refusal or inability to acknowledge or confess my lie about you.

My lie is the sin or misdeed. Its seemingly autonomous power that has marginalized you resides in the fact that it is not confessed. The situation changes if I confess the lie. If I let it be known to all concerned that what they heard about you was a lie, the situation changes. The community regains control. To be sure, the community must now decide what to do about me. The consequences for me could be quite severe, but the community is now in control. Confession controls evil. It undermines its power.

Within partnership ways, confession is not the guilt inducing enterprise it has become under morality and the dominator system. It is not designed to paralyze someone with guilt. Instead, it is one of the most important tools in the struggle against evil. As the illustrations above reveal, evil's opposition to life is undermined the moment a person, group or nation acknowledges a sin or misdeed. Healing takes place. To be sure, there is still work to do, but the seemingly autonomous force in opposition to life called evil ceases to exist.

As the story of David and Bathsheba indicates, it is one thing when *individuals* refuse to acknowledge and confess their sins or misdeeds. The consequences are far more severe when groups, communities, religions and nations refuse to confess. The recent pedophilia of a number of Roman Catholic priests illustrates both the extent of the evil created by unconfessed sin as well as how confession is abused by morality and the forces of domination. What is even more damaging than the individual priestly crimes is the fact that these crimes were known but not confessed by the institutional church for so many years. Bishops, Arch-Bishops and Cardinals knew the crimes. Their response was a cover-up. They silenced their victims. They merely relocated the culprits to other parishes where many offenders continued their crimes against humanity in new settings. In its refusal to confess its sin, the Church hierarchy unleashed evil with all its deadly force. The damage done to the Church, the world and most especially the young victims is beyond measure. This damage, however, is a direct consequence of the evil unleashed by the refusal to confess. A quick and timely confession of these sins to the community and the world would have prevented so much destruction.

This is all the more tragic because it happened within an institution that should have known that confession fights evil. The

Roman Catholic Church, however, did not know this because, like most of Christianity, it serves the dominator system. Accordingly, it stresses morality rather than ethics. As a consequence, the Roman Catholic Church relegated confession and absolution to a sacrament that serves the dominant world view. In accord with civilization's world view, the purpose of confession and absolution is to reestablish the absolved one on the proper side of the moral divide. In many instances, this understanding of confession *enabled* evil. It did not fight evil. When it serves the partnership worldview, however, confession is an effective way to combat evil.

In July of 2008, the Pope apologized for the sexual abuses of Roman Catholic priests. It is probably true to say that the Pope was acting in accord with partnership ways when he did so. It is also true to say that his apology (I don't think Popes actually confess to the world) was quite untimely. Evil had an opportunity to flourish because the abuse of boys remained an unconfessed sin in the Church for so long. In short, the more timely a confession is, the less damage is done. There would have been less abuse and less psychological damage had the Roman authorities confessed these sins in a timely manner and made amends within the priesthood itself. As long as a sin or misdeed is not acknowledged or confessed, it is the source of the seemingly autonomous force against life called evil. Once evil is unleashed to do its damage, we must live with its consequences. Confession allows us to stop evil, but confession cannot change the past. King David's confession to the prophet Nathan did not change history. Uriah was still dead. His loyal men were robbed of their lives as well. Likewise, the Pope's apology or confession could not undue the damage done before the sin was confessed. To use the Treaty of Versailles as another example of untimely confession, following World War II the allies did note some of the injustices of the Treaty of Versailles. Indeed, the Marshall Plan was an effort to avoid the mistakes of the Treaty of Versailles. Nonetheless, we still live with the consequences of our refusal or inability to acknowledge and confess the allied misdeeds at Versailles. Had the allies acknowledged and confessed their own sins or misdeeds in bringing about the World War I, World War II might have been avoided. Without World War II, nuclear power might not have been discovered, and we would not be living under the threat of nuclear obliteration. Timely confessions are much better than untimely ones because they prevent the emergence of evil – the seemingly autonomous force in opposition to life.

The Misappropriation of Ethical Virtues and Tactics

The ability to misappropriate and abuse ethical virtues and tactics reveals the strength of the dominator system. The tragic consequences of the priestly acts of sexual abuses in the Roman Catholic Church are illustrative. Here the dominator system uses confession quite differently. Under the dominator system, confession is not a way that evil is fought. It is a way that a person re-establishes himself or herself on the "good" side of the moral divide. The sexual abuse of a child places the one performing the act on the "evil" side of the moral divide. The act is confessed and absolved. The culprit is restored to the "good" side of the moral divide, and the culprit is allowed to continue his death-dealing activities. In other words, the dominator system uses confession to promote its death-dealing work. Under the control of the dominator system, confession is not a way to fight evil. It is a way of perpetuating evil.

Other ethical virtues receive the same fate when usurped by the dominator system and morality. Humility can be used to reinforce the hierarchies that morality and the dominator system perpetuate. It is one thing for the master to counsel his servants to be humble. It is another for the master himself to be humble. When servants, slaves or employees heed their masters' admonition to be humble, humility is being used to perpetuate the death dealing tactics of the dominator system because such humility preserves the masters' status and perpetuates the hierarchy. As a virtue of partnership, humility is an ethical virtue meant to combat the arrogance of the rich, the powerful and the educated. If it is misappropriated by the dominator system, it merely perpetuates hierarchy.

One way to resist morality's ability to usurp ethical virtues and tactics is to ask the question, "Who is speaking?" "Who is the one telling you to be humble or to forgive or act mercifully?" One of the most important, but largely overlooked, aspects of the Ten Commandments themselves is their introduction. "I am the Lord your God who emancipated you from the Land of Egypt, you shall have no other gods before me." The Ten Commandments would be perceived quite differently if this introduction were different. If it had said, "I am Pharaoh, you shall have no other gods before me," or "I am Adolph Hitler, you shall have no other gods before me," the meaning of the Ten Commandments would be quite different.

Now I will just bet that you are thinking that it actually does not make any difference who uttered the Ten Commandments. If you are, this betrays your allegiance to the dominator system. The dominator system has led us to believe that the Ten Commandments are universal moral truths. It does not matter who says, "You shall not kill" or "You shall not steal." These are universal truths. This is patently false. It is one thing for the one who liberated you from slavery to say, "You shall not steal." It is quite another for a slave owner to say, "You shall not steal." The slave owner is the one who has already stolen the slave from herself. Indeed, if a slave were to run away, she would be stealing herself from her master at least according to the dictates of morality and the dominator system. The words, "You shall not steal" coming from the master's lips are moral dictates designed to perpetuate the injustices of slavery. The words, "You shall not steal" coming from the lips of the one who liberated you from slavery are boundary words. In other words, they establish the limits of partnership ways. For example, a community that routinely kills – like Nazi Germany - cannot be a partnership community. A community that routinely covets – a consumer society relies on covetousness to survive – cannot be a partnership community. A community that routinely bears false witness against neighbors – like Stalin's Soviet Union – cannot be a partnership community. The Ten Commandments establish these boundaries.

It is in the interest of the dominator system to divorce the Ten Commandments from the one who liberated the Israelites from their slavery in Egypt because this makes the Ten Commandments moral dictates. As moral dictates the Ten Commandments perpetuate the dominator system's hierarchical order. This is why there is so much interest by many of our political leaders to place the Ten Commandments in public places. But if the Ten Commandments originate in the one who liberated people from slavery, they are much different. They are boundary words that demonstrate the limits of partnership cultures.

The actual literary context of the Ten Commandments indicates that these commandments are not meant to be moral absolutes, but instead are meant to establish the boundaries of a new sort of community. In our discussion of how ethics are communal rather than individualistic, we mentioned Jethro's administrative reform. When Moses' father-in-law Jethro brought Moses' wife and children, he saw that Moses was the sole authority among the recently emancipated Israelites. He said to Moses, "What you are doing is *not good*. You and the people with you will wear yourselves out, for the thing is too heavy for you; you are not able to perform it alone." (Ex. 18: 17, 18). Jethro then told Moses to appoint leaders among the people. Some should judge over 1000 people. Others should judge over hundreds, fifties and tens. These judges should address the easier disputes and leave the hard ones for Moses. We have already discussed the new sort of community that this reform created. We have not discussed the fact that Jethro's administrative reform begins with the words, "What you are doing is *not good*."

The words, "not good" echo Genesis 2:18 where God says, "It is *not good* that the man should live alone." In this instance, Claus Westermann argues that the word good does not mean some fixed and objective standard of measuring morality. Instead, good means suited for a particular purpose for which it is being prepared. "It corresponds to a goal."[20] If something is *not good*, that thing is not suited for the purpose for which it is intended. When God says, "It is *not good* that the man should live alone," God is saying that if Adam remains alone, God cannot do what God intended to do with Adam. Likewise, when Jethro says what Moses is doing is *not good*, Jethro is commenting on the Israelite's organizational structure. As it stands, this structure is incompatible with the purpose of a community that is to be an alternative to the dominate society. Accordingly, a different way to order society was developed by Jethro and implemented by Moses.

It is an extremely significant literary fact that when Moses climbed Mt. Sinai to receive the Ten Commandments, he did so on behalf of a community that was organized as an alternative to the nations and empires that surrounded Israel. This was not a dominator nation. It was an alternative to the dominate cultures. Furthermore, these commandments were given by the One who had emancipated this alternative community from slavery. These are extremely significant but generally overlooked facts. These literary facts are overlooked because they subvert our normal understanding of the Ten Commandments which understands the Ten Commandments as absolute moral standards. They are not absolute moral standards, and they were never meant to be. Only the dominator system and its morality demand that they be so. Instead the Ten Commandments are boundary statements. Partnership communities are not possible if things like killing, adultery, false witness and coveting are routine.

The commandments are generally divided into two tables. The first introduces the speaker and concerns the worship of God, God's name and God's day.

> I am the Lord your God who emancipated you from slavery in Egypt.

> You shall have no other Gods before me.

> Do not make images and worship them.

> Do not use the name of the Lord your God in vain.

> Remember the Sabbath and keep it Holy.

The second table contains commandments that concern the nature of Israel's alternative community.

> Honor your mother and father that your days may be long in the land I am giving you.

> Do not kill.

> Do not commit adultery.

> Do not steal.

> Do not bear false witness against your neighbor.

> Do not covet another's wife, slave, cattle, donkey or anything else he owns.[21]

The following discussion begins with the second table. It often goes unnoticed, but, with the exception of the commandment, "honor your mother and father," these commandments are all negative. They tell us what *not* to do. They say little if anything about what to do. We are commanded not to kill, but we are not told how to live with the people we do not kill. That seems to be left to our imagination. We are commanded to refrain from adultery. Perhaps this is a commandment designed to protect our own family and the families of others. This commandment, however, gives us no idea of what a family is. (Today a guy like Israel's patriarch Jacob would be arrested for having the sort of family he had). We are commanded not to steal, but there is no guide concerning how we are to treat another person's property. There is not even a guide to what constitutes property. (Many Native Americans, for example, did not think it possible to own land. For them owning land itself was stealing. Indeed, from the perspective of Native Americans, the Pope, Portugal and Spain pulled off the greatest theft of land the world has known with the Treaty of Tordesillas in 1494. Here the Pope divided the lands of North and South America between the Portuguese and the Spanish.[22] How the Pope came to own these lands in order that he might divide them remains mysterious to American Indians to this day.) We are commanded not to speak falsely about our neighbor, but we are told neither how to speak about our neighbor nor who our neighbor is. Finally, we are told not to covet. We are not told what our attitude toward the possessions of another should be.

The negative aspects of these commandments leave open a wide variety of possible actions. The community might find that it is important to create rules governing such behavior, but these rules will always be contextual. That is to say, they exist because of the perceived needs of their community of origin. They are not meant to be universal. They govern only the life of the community in which they are developed.

The Commandments did not create Israel. Israel was created when the Israelites were emancipated from Egypt. The Commandments exist to protect Israel and perhaps other alternative communities. To be sure, they did not protect Israel from foreign invasion. They protected Israel from itself.[23] The Ten Commandments marked the boundaries of this alternative community called Israel. That is to say, the alternative community of Israel would die if Israel routinely violated these commandments.

This is not exactly a threat. God was not saying Israel would die *because* it routinely violated the commandments. It is more a statement of limits or boundaries. It is saying that if Israel – or perhaps any alternative community – disregards these commandments, it simply will not be an alternative to the dominator model. Every expression of the dominator model routinely violates one or more of these commandments. For example, Rome, the Soviet Union and Nazi Germany routinely violated the commandment against killing. The United States routinely violates the commandment against coveting because coveting fuels its economic system. Because of these routine violations, Rome, the Soviet Union, Nazi Germany and the United States are not alternative communities. Alternative communities do not exist if they too routinely violate one or more of these commandments.

There is one final and debatable question about the second table of commandments. Can they stand alone? Do they need divine support? On the one hand, many people – atheist and theist alike – think that the commandments are or should be universal moral absolutes. They believe they are universal. These people, however, understand the Ten Commandments within the context of civilization and the dominator system. As we have seen, in practice, there is no universal morality in civilizations under the dominator system. To be sure, each civilization thinks that its own moral code ought to be universal, but there has never been a moral code universal to all human beings. Indeed, rather than promoting absolutes like "You shall not kill," most moral codes justify the killing of those marginalized by morality itself. We have already discussed such matters.

The real question is "Does the second table of commandments need divine support within a partnership framework?" Suffice it to say, the first table of commandments introduced a God who emancipated Israel from its bondage to Egypt's version of the dominator system. Accordingly, these first commandments held out hope to Israel. Quite frankly, it is not all that obvious that partnership will triumph over morality and civilization. The first table helped Israel realize that they were not alone in their attempt to create an alternative community and live in accord with ethics and partnership. While it is clear that alternative communities have been and can be developed apart from belief in Israel's God (or any god), it must be emphasized that Israel was very conscious of the dominator system's powerful opposition to its alternative experiment. Israel's God gave them hope when facing such opposition. It reminded the people that they are not on their own in their efforts to form alternatives to morality and the dominator system. In this day and age, the dominator system is even more formidable. It is so powerful that it made a near successful attempt to destroy the Jewish people themselves. In my opinion, (and this may be heretical) the Holocaust demonstrates the awesome death-dealing power of the dominator system. It is so powerful, that the God who liberated Israel from Egypt might not be powerful enough to withstand its death-dealing power.

Nonetheless, one need not be a believer to recognize the advantage the assistance of a God might be in opposing a force as powerful as the dominator system. It is in this way that the first table of the Ten Commandments supports the second within the partnership framework. Some may not think that there is a God who supports partnership ways, but the struggle is so profound that even they might admit they could use the help.

Social and Individual Ethics

Ethics can be divided into two realms: individual ethics and social ethics. With the possible exception of Biblical prophets like Amos and Jeremiah who recognized the relationship between ancient Israel's social and religious structures and poverty, social ethics is a very recent phenomenon. It recognizes that our social structures are of human origin, therefore, subject to criticism.

Excepting the prophets of Israel, the Bible and most pre-modern ethical thought concerned individual ethics. The Apostle Paul, for example, stated that in Christ there is neither Jew nor Gentile, slave or free, male or female, but he never directly attacked the institution of slavery or the subjugation of women. At best, the Apostle would send a slave back to his master telling the master to receive the slave as a brother in Christ (Philemon). In other words, Paul tried to change the attitude of the master toward his slave or the husband toward the wife, but he had little to say about the institution of slavery, and he seemed to think that patriarchy was ordained by God. Accordingly, he remained on the level of individual ethics. He never moved into the field of social ethics by challenging the institution of slavery or the patriarchy that dominated his civilization. For centuries ethics was confined to individual ethics. Slavery, racism, sexism were thought to be givens of nature or divinely ordained; hence, these social structures were not themselves subject to critique.

Recognizing that the social orders of civilization and culture were of human origin was the first step in the emergence of social ethics. The fifth chapter was largely an inquiry into social ethics. Indeed, it challenged the actual design of civilization itself. It maintained that the basic social design of civilization was lodged in the agricultural revolution's most fundamental technology, namely, the commoditization of food. The commoditization of food demanded that moral (not ethical) criteria be developed to determine who was worthy of food and who was not. This need to establish a person's worthiness to receive food provides the basic structure of civilization to this day. We have seen how it demands the moral divide be draw between good and evil. This divide dominates our political and religious life. The moral divide led to ranking and hierarchy – which are two inescapable elements of our civilizations. I have speculated that the very moment food was commoditized criteria were developed that established who was worthy of food and who was not. This was the origin of morality. Priests sanctified morality – our various understandings of good and evil – when they made it appear these arbitrary criteria were god-given. These sanctified values led to ranking the good ones over the evil ones and the best ones over the merely good. This is the source of hierarchy and the dominator system that appears to be behind most civilizations.

Moreover, morality – our knowledge of good and evil – is death-dealing. I argued that Nazi Germany's death-dealing tactics were consistent with morality and civilization, and not the immoral or uncivilized anomaly most of us wishfully say they were. Nazi Germany was not inevitable. It did not have to happen. Nonetheless, Nazi Germany was consistent with the principles of morality and civilization. Indeed, it is a demonic archetype of the death-dealing tactics implicit in civilization and morality. Civilization has provided a number of lesser but still death-dealing examples of how death emerges from morality and civilization. The brutality of the Roman Empire, the slaughter of medieval heretics, the destruction of the indigenous population of the New World, slavery or apartheid disclose how engrained the practices of Nazi Germany are in the structure of civilization and its morality.

For the most part, this chapter was devoted to individual ethics. I argued that communal power, confession, forgiveness, listening, humility and mercy are ethical virtues associated with the practice of life. I called these partnership or life virtues because their practice allows us to obtain goods internal to the practice of life. In one sense they are individual virtues, hence, the subject of individual ethics. In another sense, however, they span the distinction between social and individual ethics because *the use of any partnership virtue creates a partnership episode that lasts as long as the virtue is performed.* In other words, partnership happens when communal power is employed. Partnership happens when people listen, forgive, and act with humility. These virtues create new ways of living when enacted. The longer they are practiced, the longer partnership happens.

Chapter 7:

Beyond What We Are

> "Do not fail to notice the significance of all tyrannies today describing themselves as democracies, and all conquests as liberations and all arbitrariness as the people's justice. This already is a great victory of light over darkness and a great step forward from the Machiavellian approval of every kind of political crime."
>
> E.F. Schumacher.[1]

Ethics and morality are different because they operate in different contexts. Morality is reasoned behavior that supports civilization. Ethics is reasoned behavior that sustains life. It is important to change from the dominator worldview to a partnership world view because civilization as it now exists is not sustainable. Dominator virtues are leading us to destruction. I hope this is not true, but I think it is. Under the civilized, dominator paradigm we look to technological innovations to save us from what would otherwise be a grim future; yet, the same people who look to technology for hope also know that technological innovations create as many problems as they solve. Our pessimism about the future is demonstrated by the fact that we rarely think beyond the next generation. Absent major technological innovations many people doubt we will survive the next century or two. Some express the deranged hope to die before all our resources are gone. This may be because we sense the relationship between morality and death expressed in the ancient story of the Garden of Eden.

Alternatives are possible. Culture is possible without civilization. Ethics is possible without morality. Alternatives emerge the moment we refuse to acknowledge the moral divide that civilization establishes between the good and the evil; the worthy and the unworthy; the saved and the damned. Alternatives will become clearer when we actually identify with those marginalized and left for dead by these moral demarcations. Alternatives emerge because we welcome the stranger when we identify with the marginalized. Welcoming the stranger opens us to new possibilities. Just as nature creates new possibilities for itself through symbiotic relationships between diverse life forms, so we can create new cultural possibilities through contact with other different human beings. In doing so, alternatives can be found if we establish communities that are different from the dominant civilization. Such communities jettison the virtues associated with civilization and the dominator system: unilateral power, one way communication, justification and mastery. Instead they promote partnership virtues like: communal power, listening, confession, humility and forgiveness. These partnership values and virtues are not utopian dreams. They have been practiced from the beginning of life itself. Life needs these virtues to be practiced and cannot sustain itself without them. The long history of partnership that predates the emergence of civilization demonstrates that ethics is possible without morality and that culture is possible without conforming to the particular sort of culture we now call civilization.

We have seen that ethics is practiced by two sorts of people. The first and most ancient practiced with little if any knowledge of the dominator system, morality or civilization. People who lived before the agricultural revolution are obviously in this group, but more contemporary cultures like the Iroquois Confederacy are included as well. Ethical virtues and tactics differed between these groups because each group tried to live in harmony with nature, and the character of nature differs from place to place.

While differences in nature are easy to see with respect to the Amazon and the Arctic, recent theories have suggested that the cultural differences between Indian tribes living on the Eastern coast of North America in the 16th and 17th centuries are a consequence of the fact that each tribe occupied a different watershed.[2] The differences between the natural environments of each North American watershed are much more subtle than those between the Arctic and the Amazon, but they are different enough to create several distinct American Indian cultures. In any case, attempts to live in accord with nature led these cultures to develop their own particular understandings of life.

Perverting the Legacy of the Ethical Leaders

This book has tried to use the teachings of American Indians, but it is written for those of us who have been subjects of the dominator system. As previously mentioned, it is incumbent upon those who once lived outside the influence of the dominator system *to remember* how they lived, but it is incumbent upon those within the dominator system to repent and resist the dominator system. Resistance begins when we awaken from our slumber and begin to understand the death-dealing character of morality. We have recognized a number of models for this sort of activity. Socrates resisted the moral design imposed on him by his Athenian culture when he questioned those things his culture deemed sacred. The prophets of Israel did the same thing with respect to the monarchies under which they lived. The prophetic record indicates that Israel's prophets "spoke truth to power." They challenged the monarchies of Israel, Judah, Babylonia, Persia, Greece or the Roman Empire. Moses, of course, challenged the Egyptian Pharaoh. Amos challenged Israel's king and the rich people of Israel. Jeremiah prophesied against Judah's monarchy and the Temple cult which was central to Judah's religious life. The prophet we call 2nd Isaiah questioned Babylon's worldview when the Jews were exiled in Babylonia. Daniel did the same when Israel was subject to Persian rule. In India, Siddhartha (Buddha) challenged the caste structure of Hinduism. In our modern times, people like Emma Goldman questioned nearly every governmental authority's understanding of good and evil. She is unique because she was exiled from both the United States and the Soviet Union. Gandhi, Martin Luther King and Malcolm X continue this list of people who challenge what their religion and society deem sacred.[3]

It has been the case that those who follow people like Jesus or Socrates grant these men and women sacred status, and, in the process, distort the message of their teachers. Socrates, for example, was systemically distorted by Plato. Plato himself testifies to the fact that, for Socrates, there was nothing in the state that was sacred or beyond criticism. For Plato, the Philosopher King was beyond criticism because Plato thought only the Philosopher King knew what was good and right. This is a consequence of Plato exchanging Socrates' ethical virtues for the dominator system's moral virtues. Socrates clearly practiced the ethical virtue of humility. For him the practice of philosophy began with the acknowledgment of his own ignorance. For Plato, on the other hand, the Philosopher King was not ignorant at all. Indeed, the Philosopher King approached divine status. He or she was nearly omniscient and clearly omnipotent. No one could question the Philosopher King. In contrast, Socrates understood the philosopher to be a gadfly or a necessary nuisance. As Karl Popper has said, "It is hard, I think, to conceive of a greater contrast between the Socratic and Platonic ideal of a philosopher. It is the contrast between two worlds. . . ."[4] Popper goes on to say that these two worlds are the Socratic world of a modest, rational individualist and the Platonic world of a totalitarian demigod. I would say that there are indeed two worlds in contrast here. They are the Socratic world of partnership and ethics and the Platonic world of domination and morality.

Plato distorted the philosophy of his teacher Socrates, and perhaps Western philosophy itself, by removing Socrates from a partnership/ethical paradigm and then inserting him into a dominator/moral/hierarchical framework. The same can be said of the Church and Jesus of Nazareth. The Church also distorted Jesus by removing him from his partnership/ethical paradigm and inserting him into a dominator/moral/hierarchical framework. This sort of "assimilation" is the way the dominator system routinely deals with its radical critics. In the past, the dominator system has made a religion or a systematic philosophy out of such critics. In the present, the dominator system often assimilates those who challenge what society conceives by commemorating their lives with a holiday. The United States, for example, is now in the process of remembering Martin Luther King Jr. with a holiday. When this holiday is marked by shopping more than remembrance and service, Martin Luther King Jr. will have finally been assimilated into the American version of the dominator system. In my opinion, we human beings may finally be in the position to resist this tendency. We are at the end of our moral sleepwalk and at the dawn of a new sort of consciousness.

A Reason to Hope?

In every generation there have been people who have cri-tiqued the dominant culture. We have mentioned Jesus, Socrates, Israel's prophets and Siddhartha. One might also mention people like St. Patrick who was the first person to challenge the validity of the entire institution of slavery (a man who the dominator system wants us to remember by consuming mass quantities of green beer).[5] Nonetheless, this awakening became more corporate in the nineteenth century. One would not be wrong to discuss the women's movement, socialism, Marxism, the labor movement, or the abolitionist movement as illustration of this emerging consciousness. To avoid the idea that this new consciousness is a consequence of the innate superiority of modern people to those who came before us, one might also note that this new consciousness could have emerged because of the availability of certain foods.

It is important to recall the seminal work of Jared Dia-mond that was mentioned in the introduction.[6] While most of the world has accounted for the inequalities between people and civilizations in terms of superior qualities allegedly possessed by members of the dominant group, Diamond accounted for these inequalities in terms of geography and environment. He argues cultural advantages are a consequence of an abundance of certain plants and animals – plants and animals capable of being domesticated - in certain geographical locales like China and the Fertile Crescent. It was environmental factors such as these, rather than innate human qualities, that gave certain civilizations advantages over other civilizations.

In his commentary of E.F. Schumacher's book *Good Work*, Peter Gillingham has argued in a similar manner regarding our current situation.[7] He notes that better nutrition may be playing a role in the emergence of a new consciousness in many human beings. For example, "it has become widely known and accepted that when the diet of a child in the first five years of life (or the diet of a mother before birth) has been significantly deficient in protein, particularly some of the amino acids, the individual's intelligence will be impaired, probably permanently."[8] The person in question does not become a fool or anything like that. It is just that his or her abilities to think abstractly, analytically and imaginatively is somewhat undermined if certain dietary needs are not met in the first five years of life.

Gillingham goes on to note that for most of human history our diets were generally deficient in these needed proteins. Only the nobility had access to diets with sufficient proteins. This changed in some places on the globe in the late 18th and early 19th centuries, and this change sparked a change in consciousness. Prior to this change in diet, those who acted in human history were few, and those who were acted upon were many. The change in diet and the subsequent mental capacities this fostered created more actors. This is reflected in the rise of democracy, labor unions, the women's movement, the grange movement and a whole host of social activities and ideologies that served to expand our "sense of the possible."[9]

The expansion of our intellectual capabilities, however, is not necessarily a positive thing (if positive means life-affirming). The issue is how do we use these expanded abilities or within what paradigm do we employ them. Countless examples have demonstrated that our abilities can be death-dealing if employed in the context of morality and the dominator system. The Nazis, Southern slaveholders and the architects of apartheid had few protein deficiencies. They were intelligent people who employed their analytical skills within the context of the dominator system. This had dire consequences. It may take much more than an improved diet to create the sort of consciousness toward which we strive.

Ethics and the Expansion of Human Consciousness

Over one hundred years ago, Mark Twain's, *The Adventures of Huckleberry Finn,* addressed this issue. According to Mark Twain himself, the novel is a record of Huck's struggle between "a sound heart and a deformed conscience."[10] To understand what the author may have meant by that statement, the basics of the story must be told. The story takes place in the American South of the 1840's. Slavery was the norm. The white masters believed slavery was of divine origin. Slavery's high moral status was beyond dispute. Huck and Jim meet as runaways. Huck is running away from his abusive father and from two women –the Widow Douglas and her sister Miss Watson - who want to "sivilize" him. Jim is an escaped slave. He is running away from his "owner" the same Miss Watson because he heard that she was going to sell him "down the river" where Jim would work on a Plantation and never see his family again. The story might be viewed as a quest for freedom. They leave their Missouri homes and travel down the Mississippi River in search of Cairo, Illinois where Jim hopes to head up the Ohio River to freedom.

Many of their adventures happen after they miss Cairo and continue their "escape" down the Mississippi deeper and deeper into the hostile South. Much of the story concerns Huck's conflicting emotions and thoughts regarding the escaping slave Jim. Huck knows he is helping Jim to escape, and *he knows this is wrong.* He knows this because he has been taught by every adult and every "good" and "decent" person he knew that helping a slave escape is stealing, and stealing is against God's command. In other words, the morality of slavery informed Huck's conscience, and what he learned from morality contradicted his friendship and love for Jim.

While this moral dilemma is present throughout Huck's relationship with Jim, it became acute when Jim is finally captured. Huck thought that it was good and right that Jim should be captured and returned to Jim's "owner." His conscience informed him that this was the good and decent thing to do. Yet, Huck loved Jim. He could not bear to have the man who had been both a father and a friend thrown back into slavery.

> The more I studied about this, the more my conscience went to grinding me, and the more

wicked and low-down and ornery I got to feeling. And at last, when it has me all of a sudden
that here was the plain hand of Providence slap-
ping me in the face and letting me know my
wickedness was being watched all the time from
up there in heaven, whilst I was stealing a poor
old woman's (slave) that hadn't ever done me no
harm, and now was showing me there's One
that's always on the lookout, and ain't agoing to
allow no such miserable doings to go only just
fur and no further. . . . Well, I tried the best I
could to kinder soften it up for myself, by saying
I was brung up wicked, and so I arn't so much to
blame; but something inside of me kept saying,
"There was the Sunday school, you could a gone
to it; and if you'd a done it they'd a lernt you,
there, that people that acts as I'd been acting. . .
goes to everlasting fire. . . .

I went on thinking. . . . I see Jim before me, all
the time, in the day, and in the night-time, sometimes moonlight, sometimes storms, and we a
floating along, talking, and singing, and laugh-
ing. But somehow I couldn't seem to strike no
places to harden me against him, but only the
other kind. I'd see him standing my watch on
top of his'n . . . see how glad he was when I
come back out of the fog. . . .

I'd got to decide, forever, betwixt two things,
and I knowed it. I studied a minute, sort of hold-
ing my breath, and then says to myself: "All
right, then, I'll *go* to hell."

. . . . And for a starter, I would go to work and
steal Jim out of slavery again; and if I could
think up anything worse, I would do that too;
because as along as I was in, and in for good, I
might as well go the whole hog.[11]

The *Adventures of Huckleberry Finn* addresses one of
Western civilization's unresolved issues, namely, freedom. On one
level, it is a novel about Jim's freedom. Jim's freedom is

extremely problematic in the story because Jim's freedom becomes more and more precarious as the two proceed down the Mississippi further into the slave-holding South. In Huck we see a different dimension in this same quest. Huck needs to be emancipated from the conventions of his culture just as Jim needs to be freed from the slave-holders. Huck's freedom is synonymous with his freedom from morality. He is in conflict because his conscience – a conscience formed by the morality of his slave-holding civilization – seeks to prevent him from acting on behalf of life. He had to choose between his love of Jim and his adherence to the death-dealing moral system of the American South.

The book ends with Jim being emancipated from his bondage. Given subsequent history, the reader knows that this is only the first step in Jim's freedom; nonetheless, it is an enormous step. Huck, however, is another story. At no point in the story does Huck even question the validity of his moral conventions. At no point is he conscious enough to think that perhaps it is the system instead of him that is awry. At every point he thinks he is on the evil side of the divide drawn by his civilization's morality. He believes he is damned. Huck is in bondage to morality. Even though he acts on behalf of life when he frees Jim, his conscience – a conscience given him by the moral conventions of his culture – indicts him. He stands condemned because he is unable to critically evaluate his culture. At the books end, Huck remains on the run. "But I reckon I got to light out for the Territory ahead of the rest, because Aunt Sally she's going to adopt me and sivilize me and I can't stand it. I been their before."[12]

Like most Americans, Huck mistakenly believes that freedom is just beyond the next ridge, but this is not where freedom reigns. If Mark Twain is correct, freedom entails waking up from our moral sleepwalk and becoming conscious of the death-dealing aspects of our morality. Huck never does this. Huck never wakes up. Huck never becomes conscious of the root of his dilemma. Huck's dilemma is the same as that of nearly all civilized people. Can we awaken from our moral slumber? Can we expand our consciousness to include a critique of the death-dealing tactics of our morality and overcome morality's death-dealing function?

Ironically, the horror of the Holocaust could be an event that has expanded our consciousness in this direction. (This is not an attempt to justify the Holocaust. It is just an attempt to say what happened after this horror). According to George M. Fredrickson, events of the Holocaust were so horrendous that they awakened Western civilization to the evils of racism. Racism could not withstand its absolute horror. Indeed, the Holocaust is so indefensible that even the Neo-Nazis themselves deny that it happened rather than defend or justify it.[13]

Our knowledge of the Holocaust began the process of toppling racist regimes. The next to fall after Nazi Germany was the racist regimes of the American South. In 1944, Gunnar Myrdal's book *An American Dilemma* prophetically and succinctly stated this issue. "The War (World War II) is crucial for the future of the Negro, and the Negro problem is crucial in the War. There is bound to be a redefinition of the Negro's status in America as a result of the War. . . . not since Reconstruction has there been more reason to anticipate fundamental changes in American race relations, changes which will involve a development toward the American ideals."[14]

It took over 20 years, but America did make significant progress. Congress passed voting and civil rights legislation in 1964 and 1965. In 1967, the Supreme Court nullified state laws banning intermarriage between the races. There are still many laws on the books that prove to be racist, and our prisons house a disproportionate number of African Americans and other so called "minorities." There are still racist people in the United States, but, in some cases, there are laws against racist acts. To a large extent our reaction to the horrors of the Holocaust raised our consciousness of the death-dealing force of racism. We began to find racism's death-dealing tactics intolerable.

> . . . African Americans and other traditional or potential victims of racial discrimination, not only in the United States but throughout the world gained a measure of international sympathy and even protection. The United Nation's Universal Declaration of Human Rights and Convention on the Prevention and Punishment of Crime and Genocide did not prevent the occurrence of racial injustice or even the mass murder of racial or ethnic Others, but it increased the chance that some-

thing might be done about violations of what were now international norms.[15]

With respect to racism, our consciousness has expanded on a Global scale. The last racist regime, the Union of South Africa, could not withstand this global rejection of racism. Eventually it fell because of this expansion of consciousness. We are no longer like Huck Finn who could not critique the racist system under which he lived, however, we have yet to expand our consciousness to recognize the death-dealing character of morality.

Consciousness involves comprehension and comprehension is the "unpremeditated, attentive facing up to and resistance of reality – whatever that may be."[16] This book has been about comprehending and therefore resisting morality. It awakens us from our moral slumber. The first step is to recognize that morality differs from civilization to civilization. What is "good" in one civilization might even be counted "evil" in another. Those who remain in a moral stupor normally do not resist. Accordingly, they lack comprehension. Instead, they understand their own civilization's conception of good and evil as absolute and try to impose their values on the rest of the world. In contrast, those who are beginning to awaken from their moral slumbers have begun to realize that the imposition of such absolutes actually causes or justifies much of the world's unnecessary carnage. We are slowly beginning to see that serving life involves the rejection of such absolute moral thinking.

Slowly a new consciousness emerges. We begin to understand that although the content of morality differs from place to place, the function of morality (what morality does) is absolute and universal. Morality *always* divides those it designates "good" from those it designates "evil." Next, morality *always* marginalizes and frequently *kills* those it designates "evil." Frequently, but not always, morality justifies people who both marginalize and kill those they deem unfit.

Our consciousness expands even further when we become aware of the differences between ethics and morality. We understand that morality always marginalizes someone, and we realize that ethics identifies with those morality has marginalized. Whereas Nazi morality marginalized the Jews, ethics demands identification with the Jews. Whereas South African apartheid and North American Jim Crow laws marginalized people of color, ethics demands identification with people of color. Whereas capitalism tends to marginalize the poor, ethics identifies with the poor.

We awaken all the more when we employ ethical tactics and virtues. We use communal power and abandon unilateral power. We forgive and act mercifully. We are humble rather than arrogant. Understanding others has a priority over being understood by others. We oppose evil by confessing our mistakes, misdeeds and even sins. We refrain from self-justification. If we recognize the fatal truths about morality, hierarchy and domination, and if we practice the virtues and tactics of ethics we create new, vital relationships and communities. These new creations often give further insight into the ways of ethics and partnership.

It is possible to wake up from our moral slumber. We can expand our consciousness. It is difficult. It takes a great deal of discipline, but it is not an impossible or hopeless task. In recent years there is some evidence that a new paradigm is emerging. Human beings are beginning to understand that we are part of nature and not its masters. We have become increasingly conscious of our role in the world's environmental change and have in some cases reversed environmental damage. We are becoming increasingly conscious of the fact that war is our choice and not inevitable. We are becoming conscious that societies can change without violence. We are becoming conscious of the value of caregivers for the nurture and support of life. Perhaps a new paradigm is emerging. Perhaps this discussion assists its emergence.

Appendix

Morality in Contrast to Ethics

Morality	Ethics
Draws Moral Divide between Good and Evil	Supports life in denying the moral divide
Sanctifies the good	Questions the "holiness" of those deemed good
Defines and marginalizes those on the evil side of the moral divide	Identifies with those marginalized by the moral divide
Orders society hierarchically	Society organized organically
Thinks hierarchically	Relational thinking
Uses diversity in nature and human beings to justify hierarchical design	Realizes that diversity enriches life
Employs Unilateral Power	Communal Power
One way communication	Listening
Mastery	Humility
Self-justification	Confession
Blame	Forgiveness and Mercy

Bibliography

Arendt, Hannah, *Eichmann in Jerusalem*. New York. 1963.

_____, *The Origins of Totalitarianism*. New York. 1951.

Bauman, Zygmunt. *Modernity and the Holocaust*. Maldun, MA. 1989.

_____. *Postmodern Ethics*. Malden, MA. 1993.

Bloom, Allan. Editor and translator. *The Republic of Plato*. New York. 1968.

Bonhoeffer, Dietrich. *Ethics*. New York. 1955.

Brueggemann, Walter. *David's Truth*. Philadelphia. 1986.

_____. *Genesis*. Atlanta. 1982.

Cahill, Thomas. *Desire of the Everlasting Hills*. New York. 1999.

Capra, Fritjof. *The Web of Life*. New York. 1966.

Childs, Brevard. *The Book of Exodus*. Philadelphia. 1974.

Churchill, Ward. *A Little Matter of Genocide*. San Francisco. 1997.

Copleston, Frederick. *A History of Philosophy*. Vol. I. New York. 1946

Deloria, Vine. *God is Red*. Golden, CO. 2003

Diamond, Jared. *Guns, Germs and Steel*. New York. 1999.

Drinnon, Richard. *Facing West*. Norman, OK. 1997.

Dussell, Enrique. *Ethics and Community.* Maryknoll, NY. 1986.

Eisler, Riane. *The Chalice and the Blade.* San Francisco. 1988.

_____. *The Real Wealth of Nations.* San Francisco. 2007.

Eze, Emmanuel Chukwudi. *Race and the Enlightenment.* 1997.

Fasching, Darrell J, and Dell Dechant, *Comparative Religious Ethics.* Malden, MA. 2001.

Fasching, Darrell J. *The Ethical Challenge of Auschwitz and Hiroshima.* New York, 1993.

Flander, Harold. *Rescue in Denmark.* New York. 1964.

Frederickson, George M. ed. *American Negro Slavery.* New York. 1979.

_____, *Racism.* Princeton, NJ, 2002

Galbraith, John Kenneth. *The Affluent Society.* New York. 1958.

Gustafson, Scott W. *Biblical Amnesia.* West Conshohocken, PA. 2004.

Hall, Douglas John. *Lighten Our Darkness.* Philadelphia. 1976.

Hengel, Martin. *Crucifixion in the Ancient World.* Philadelphia. 1971.

Hillberg, Raul. *The Destruction of European Jews.* New York. 1985.

Jenson, Robert W. *A Large Catechism.* Delhi, NY. 1991.

Johansen, Bruce E. *Forgotten Founders.* Ipswich, MA. 1982.

Jonas, Hans. *The Phenomenon of Life.* Evanston, IL. 1966.

Käsemann, Ernst. *Perspectives on Paul.* Philadelphia. 1971.

Laffey, Alice. *An Introduction to the Old Testament.* Philadelphia. 1988.

Levinas, Emmanuel. *Ethics and Infinity.* Pittsburgh. 1985.

Lewis, C.S. *The Lion, The Witch and The Wardrobe.* New York. 1950.

Long, Charles H. *Significations.* Aurora, CO. 1999.

Lovejoy, Arthur O. *The Great Chain of Being.* Cambridge, MA. 1936.

MacIntyre, Alasdair. *After Virtue.* Notre Dame, IN. 1984.

Mander, Jerry and Edward Goldsmith eds. *The Case Against the Global Economy.* San Francisco. 1996.

Margulis, Lynn. *Symbiotic Planet.* New York. 1998.

Margulis, Lynn and Darion Sagan. *Microcosmos.* Berkeley. 1997.

Maturana, Humberto R. and Bernhard Poerksen. *From Being to Doing.* Heidelberg. 2004.

Murphy, Gerald, ed. *The Constitution of the Iroquois Nation.* Cleveland. 1966.

Orwell, George. *1984.* New York. 1950.

Paris. Peter. *Social Teachings of the Black Churches.* Philadelphia. 1985.

Popper, Karl. *Open Society and Its Enemies.* Vol. I, II. Princeton, NJ. 1962, 1966.

Postman, Neil. *Conscientious Objections.* New York. 1988.

_____. *Technopoly.* New York, 1992.

_____. *The Disappearance of Childhood.* New York. 1994.

Quinn, Daniel, *After Dachau.* New York. 2000

_____. *Beyond Civilization.* New York. 1999

_____. *Ishmael.* New York. 1992.

_____. *My Ishmael.* New York. 1997.

_____. *The Story of B.* New York. 1996.

Reeves, Peggy. *Women at the Center.* Ithica, NY. 2002.

Ritzer, George, *The McDonaldization of Society.* Thousand Oaks, CA. 1996.

Rubenstein, Richard. *The Cunning of History.* New York. 1975.

Schlegel, Stuart. *A Wisdom from a Rain Forest.* Athens, GA. 1998.

Thiellicke, Helmut, *Theological Ethics.* Vol. I. Grand Rapids, MI. 1979.

Tinker, George E. and David E. Wilkens. *Native Voices.* Lawrence, KA. 2003.

Tinker, George E. *Missionary Conquest.* Minneapolis. 1993.

_____. *Spirit and Resistance.* Minneapolis. 2004.

Weatherford, Jack. *Indian Givers.* New York. 1988.

Westermann, Claus. *Creation.* Philadelphia. 1974.

White, Lynn. *Medieval Technology and Social Change.* New York. 1962.

Wiener, Philip P. ed. *Leibniz Selections.* New York. 1951.

Williams, Jay G. "Expository Article: Gen. 3," *Interpretation.* 1981.

Wink, Walter. *Engaging the Powers.* Minneapolis. 1992.

Zinn, Howard and Anthony Arnove. *Voices of a People's History of the United States.* New York. 2004.

Zinn, Howard. *A People's History of the United States.* New York. 1999.

Endnotes

Introduction

[1] Hannah Arendt, *The Origins of Totalitarianism* (New York: Harcourt Brace Jovanovich, 1951, 1973) p. viii.

[2] C.S. Lewis, *The Lion, The Witch and The Wardrobe* (New York: Macmillan Publishing Company, 1950).

[3] Jared Diamond, *Guns, Germs and Steel: The Fates of Human Societies* (New York: W.W. Norton and company, 1999) p. 18-20.

[4] Ibid, p. 87.

[5] Ibid, p. 141.

[6] Ibid, p. 195-214

[7] Ibid, p. 162.

[8] Ibid, p. 157-175.

[9] See Stuart Schlegel's discussion of the Teduray culture in the Philippines in Stuart Schlegel, *A Wisdom from a Rain Forest* (Athens, GA: University of Georgia Press, 1998), and Peggy Reeves Sanday's account of the 2 million strong Minangkaban culture in her book *Women at the Center: Life in a Modern Matriarchy* (Ithica, NY: Cornell University Press, 2002). In her most recent book *The Real Wealth of Nations: Creating a Caring Economics* (San Francisco: Burrett-Koehler Publishers, Inc., 2007) p. 93-116, Riane Eisler recognizes the work of these people, but does not limit this view of partnership culture to so-called primitive societies. She sees partnership culture emerging in the design of modern Nordic cultures as well.

[10] Darrell J. Fasching and Dell Dechant, *Comparative Religious Ethics: A Narrative Approach* (Malden, MA: Blackwell Publishing, 2001) p. 13-21.

[11] Ibid, p. 98-102.

[12] Ibid.

[13] Charles H. Long, *Significations: Signs, Symbols and Images in the Interpretation of Religion* (Aurora, CO: Davies Group Publishers, 1999) p. 1-9.

Chapter 1: The Dominator System and Partnership Ways

[1] Neil Postman, *Conscientious Objections: Stirring Up Trouble about Language, Technology and Education* (New York: Vintage Books, 1988)

p. 25. This quote was adjusted somewhat so as not to accept Postman's own male oriented definitions.

[2] Riane Eisler, *The Chalice and the Blade: Our History, Our Future* (San Francisco: Harper, 1988) p. 57.

[3] Ibid, p. xvii.

[4] Ibid.

[5] Instead of ranking, those who live in accord with partnership ways use place – geographical location – as the source of meaning and worth. As a consequence, partnership culture is in crisis whenever its participants are forced from their place. This is probably because partnership people live in accord with nature and nature differs from place to place. When partnership people are forced from their place, their ways may be inconsistent with nature in their new location.

[6] As quoted, Fritjof Capra, *The Web of Life: A New Scientific Understanding of Living Systems* (New York: Doubleday, 1966) p. xi.

[7] Vine Deloria Jr. *God is Red: A Native View of Religion.* Thirtieth Anniversary Edition (Golden Colorado: Fulcrum Press, 2003) p. 88.

[8] Lynn Margulis and Darion Sagan, *Microcosmos: Four Billion Years of Microbial Evolution* Berkeley: University of California Press, 1997) p. 16.

[9] Lynn Margulis, *Symbiotic Planet (A New Look at Evolution)* (New York: Basic Books, 1998) and Lynn Margulis and Darion Sagan *Microcosmos*

[10] Margulis and Sagan, *Microcosmos*, p. 75.

[11] Ibid.

[12] Ibid, p. 30.

[13] Ibid, p. 31.

[14] Ibid, p. 31, 32. Italics mine.

[15] Ibid, p. 33.

[16] Jack Weatherford, *Indian Givers: How the Indians of the Americas Transformed the World* (New York: Fawcett Books, 1988) p. 135.

[17] See for example, Bruce E. Johansen, *Forgotten Founders* (Ipswich MA: Gambit, 1982) or Jack Weatherford, *Indian Givers.* p. 133-150.

[18] *The Constitution of the Iroquois Nation: The Great Binding Law. GAYANASHAGOWA.* Prepared by Gerald Murphy and the National Public Telecomputing Network (Cleveland, OH: the Cleveland Free-Net, 1966). Hereafter only the number of the articles of this constitution will be referenced in the text.

[19] I am nervous about the use of the word "lord" in this context. Native American authors contend that the way white people translate certain words from the languages of American Indians often says more about the translator than about what is being translated. In other words, the translator may only be able to conceive of a leader as a Lord because of the translator's cultural bias. Nonetheless, I will stay with this translation throughout because I am not qualified to change it.

[20] Eisler, p. 57.

[21] For a more comprehensive treatment of this assertion see Scott W. Gustafson, *Biblical Amnesia: A Forgotten Story of Redemption, Resistance and Renewal* (West Conshohocken, PA: Infinity Publishing, 2004).

[22] Alice Laffey, *An Introduction to the Old Testament: A Feminist Perspective* (Philadelphia: Fortress Press, 1988) p. 47.

[23] Walter Brueggemann, *The Prophetic Imagination* (Philadelphia: Fortress Press, 1978) p. 11-27.

[24] George E. Tinker, *Spirit and Resistance: Political Theology and American Indian Liberation* Minneapolis: Fortress Press, 2004) p. 62-72.

[25] Eisler, *Chalice and the Blade,* p. 42, 43.

[26] Daniel Quinn develops this theory in the following novels. *Ishmael* (New York: Bantam Books, 1992). *The Story of B* (New York: Bantam Books, 1996). *My Ishmael* (New York: Bantam Books, 1997). Quinn also wrote a non-fiction account of his theory of civilization called *Beyond Civilization: Humanity's Next Great Adventure* (New York: Three Rivers Press, 1999).

[27] Quinn, *My Ishmael,* p. 61.

[28] Edward Goldsmith, "The Last Word: Family, Community and Democracy," in *The Case Against the Global Economy: (and for a turn to the local)* Edited by Jerry Mander and Edward Goldsmith (San Francisco: Sierra Club Books, 1996) p. 503, 504.

[29] For a clear demonstration of the relationship between technology and social change see Lynn White Jr. *Medieval Technology and Social Change* (New York: Oxford University Press, 1962). Neil Postman applies the thesis that technology is never socially or ideologically neutral in *Technopoly: The Surrender of Culture to Technology* (New York: Alfred A Knopf, 1992). Here Postman notes the relationship between medical technology and medical practice; writing and human memory; television and human community. Postman further explores the socio/political and institutional innovations caused by the printing press and television in *The Disappearance of Childhood* (New York: Vintage Books, 1994).

[30] Postman, *Technopoly,* p. 18.

[31] Please do not limit your understanding of technological change to an understanding of machines. Technological innovations are more often a way to think about something than they are mechanical innovations. McDonald's great technological innovation was also a new way to think about food. They invented what we now call "fast food." Moreover, the organization and thought necessary to produce "fast food" is now applied to industries as diverse as education, healthcare, and the funeral industry. George Ritzer, *The McDonaldization of Society: An Investigation into the Changing Character of Contemporary Social Life* (Thousand Oaks, CA: Pine Forge Press, 1996)

[32] Quinn, *Ishmael,* p. 151-184.

[33] Richard Drinnon, *Facing West: The Metaphysics of Indian Hating and Empire Building* (Norman: University of Oklahoma Press, 1997) p. 56-191.

[34] Quinn, *Ishmael,* p. 151-184.

Chapter 2: The Death Dealing Character of Morality

[1] Jay G. Williams, "Expository Article: Genesis 3," *Interpretation: A Journal of Biblical Theology.* Vol. 35. No. 3, 1981, p. 278.

[2] Enrique Dussell, *Ethics and Community,* translated by Robert R. Barr (Maryknoll, NY: Orbis Books, 1986) p. 50.

[3] See Zygmunt Bauman, *Modernity and the Holocaust* (Maldun, MA: Polity Press, 1989) for an interesting, well argued expression of how the Holocaust was not an exception to our moral codes and scientific belief systems. Rather the Holocaust is very consistent with our morality, sociology, technology and scientific world view. Bauman accurately notes that our morality, sociology, technology and science did not make the Holocaust inevitable, but they did establish the conditions that made it possible.

[4] Charles H. Long, *Significations: Signs, Symbols, and Images in the Interpretation of Religion* p. 115

[5] Ibid, p. xv-xvii and 89-95.

[6] Drinnon, p. 55.

[7] Ibid, 54, 55.

[8] George Tinker, *Missionary Conquest: the Gospel and Native American Cultural Genocide* (Minneapolis, MN: Fortress Press, 1993) p. 21-41.

[9] For a profound, eye opening introduction to the many things we have learned or could have learned from the indigenous populations of North and South America see Jack Weatherford, *Indian Givers.*

[10] C.S. Lewis, *The Lion, The Witch and The Wardrobe* (New York: Macmillan Publishing, 1950).

[11] Alexander Miller, "Is Everything Permitted?" *The Student World.* XXXVIII. No. 4 (1945) p. 298 as quoted Helmut Thiellicke, *Theological Ethics: Vol. I: Foundations.* Edited and translated by William H. Lazareth (Grand Rapids, MI: Eerdmanns, 1979) p. 586, 587. Italics mine.

Chapter 3: Morality and the Rationalization of Racism and Oppression

[1] Ani DiFranco, "Serpentine," *Evolve* (Buffalo, NY: Righteous Babe Records, 2003) Song # 11.

[2] Postman, *Technopoly,* p. 18.

[3] David K. Shipler, *The Working Poor: Invisible in America* (New York: Alfred A Knopf, 2004) p. 89, 90. Italics mine.

[4] Riane Eisler, *The Real Wealth of Nations,* p. 69-91.

[5] Karl Popper, *The Open Society and Its Enemies: Vol. I: The Spell of Plato* (Princeton, NJ: Princeton University Press, 1993) p. 46, 47.

[6] Ibid, p. 47.

[7] Ibid, p. 35, 36.

[8] Frederick Copleston S.J. *A History of Philosophy: Vol. I: Greece and Rome* (New York: The Newman Press, 1946) p. 232.

[9] Plato, *The Republic of Plato,* 460c. Translated by Allan Bloom (New York: Basic Books, 1968) p. 139.

[10] Copleston, p. 466-469. One important difference between Plotinus and the Christianized versions of his philosophy is the Christians described Plotinus' emanations from the *One* as creation. Plotinus probably did not believe in creation. His account of emanation was a description of an eternal, unchanging reality. It was not a sequence of historical events.

[11] Arthur O. Lovejoy, *The Great Chain of Being: A Study of the History of an Idea* (Cambridge, MA: Harvard University Press, 1936) p. 55. While Lovejoy is concerned with a far more complicated idea than hierarchy in this study, his study provides some insight into the notion that Western philosophies have never completely abandoned the assumption that reality is ordered hierarchically.

[12] Microbius, *Comment, in Somnium Scipionis* I, 14, 15. As quoted and translated, Lovejoy, p. 63.

[13] Nicolus of Cusa, *De docta ignoranti,* III, 1. As quoted and translated, Lovejoy, p. 80. Italics mine.

[14] Gottfried Wilhelm Leibniz, "Discourse on Methodology," *Leibniz Selections.* Edited by Philip P. Wiener (New York: Charles Scribners Sons, 1951) p. 290-292.

[15] Leibniz, "On the Principle of Continuity (from a letter to Varigam, 1702)" *Leibniz Selections,* p. 185.

[16] John Locke, *Essay Concerning Human Understanding* III, Ch. 6 as quoted in Lovejoy, p. 186.

[17] Carl von Linne, *The God Given Order of Nature (1778)* in *Race and the Enlightenment: A Reader,* edited by Emmanuel Chuckwudi Eze (Oxford: Blackwell Publishing, 1997) p. 10-13.

[18] Eze, p. 38.

[19] Immanuel Kant, "On the Immediate Causes of the Origins of these Different Races," in Eze, p. 48.

[20] David Hume, "Of Populous Ancient Nations (1748)" Eze, p. 33.

[21] Thomas Jefferson, *Notes on the State of Virginia* in Eze, p. 96.

[22] Ibid, p. 97-103.

[23] George M. Frederickson, "Slaves and Race: The Southern Dilemma," *American Negro Slavery: A Modern Reader* (New York: Oxford Press, 1979) p. 34-58.

[24] Ibid, p. 35.

[25] Frederickson, p. 37

[26] Ibid, p. 40.

[27] Thomas Cahill, *Desire of the Everlasting Hills: the World Before and After Jesus* (New York: Random House, 1999) p. 30, 31.

Chapter 4: The Holocaust: Morality in the Extreme

[1] Richard L. Rubenstein, *The Cunning of History: The Holocaust and the American Future* (New York: Harper Collins Publishers, 1975) p. 21

[2] Dussell, p. 49, 50

[3] See Daniel Quinn, *After Dachau* (New York: Zolan Books, 2000) for an outstanding fictional account of what human moral values would be if Nazi Germany had won the war.

[4] Bauman, *Modernity and the Holocaust* argues in much the same way and is an important source for the following moral and ethical reflections.

[5] John Kenneth Galbraith, *The Affluent Society* (New York: The New American Library, 1958) p. 31.

[6] Rubenstein, p. 7.

[7] Ibid, p. 10. Italics mine.

[8] Ibid, p. 11.

[9] Ibid, p. 16.

[10] Eze, p. 38-48.

[11] George M. Fredrickson, *Racism: A Short History* (Princeton: Princeton University Press, 2002) p. 70, 71.

[12] Karl R. Popper, *The Open Society and Its Enemies 2: Hegel and Marx* (Princeton, NJ: Princeton University Press, 1966) p. 32.

[13] Ibid, p. 31.

[14] G.W.F. Hegel, *Philosophy of Law, 331*, as quoted, ibid, p. 57.

[15] Hannah Arendt, *Eichmann in Jerusalem: A Report on the Banality of Evil* (New York: Penguin Books, 1963) p. 131.

[16] Ibid, 115.

[17] Raul Hillberg, *The Destruction of European Jews: Student Edition* (New York: Holmes and Meier, 1985) p. 303.

[18] Ibid, p. 267.

[19] Bauman, *Modernity and the Holocaust,* p. 197.

[20] Christopher R. Browning, "'The Government Experts,'" in *The Holocaust: Ideology, Bureaucracy and Genocide,* ed. Harry Friedlander and Subil Milton (Millwood, NY: Krause International Publication, 1985) p. 190 as quoted Ibid, p. 197.

[21] It is important to note that this bureaucratic mentality is not only a German phenomenon. It was quite present in the making of the atomic bomb, for example. As great as the inventors of the bomb were, very few even questioned the consequences of their actions while working on the project. Their focus – like Willy Just's focus – was on the technical task at hand. See Darrell Fasching, *The Ethical Challenge of Auschwitz and Hiroshima: Apocalypse or Utopia* (Albany, NY: New York: State University of New York Press, 1993) p. 96-100.

[22] Bauman, *Modernity and the Holocaust,* p. 12-30.

[23] Ellie Wiesel, *One Generation After* (New York: Avon Books, 1965) p. 10.

[24] Fasching, *The Ethical Challenge of Auschwitz and Hiroshima.* p. 103.

[25] Ibid, p. 191.

[26] Ibid.

[27] Howard Zinn, *A People's History of the United States: 1492 – Present* (New York: Harper and Row, 1999) p. 1023; 125-149. Ward Churchill, *A Little Matter of Genocide: Holocaust and Denial in the Americas 1492 to the Present* (San Francisco: City Lights Books, 1997) esp. p. 129-289. Richard Drinnon, *Facing West: the Metaphysics of Indian-Hating and Empire Building*, p. 3-191.

Chapter 5: Ethics without Morality

[1] Dietrich Bonhoeffer, *Ethics,* edited by Eberhard Bethge (New York: MacMillan Publishing Co. Inc., 1955) p. 17.

[2] Hans Jonas, "Gnosticism, Existentialism and Nihilism," *The Phenomenon of Life: Toward a Philosophical Biology* (Evanston, Illinois: Northwestern University Press, 1966) p. 218.

[3] Irenaeus, *Against Heresies,* Bk. IV, Ch XXXVIII.1 in *The Ante-Nicene Fathers,* Vol. I (Grand Rapids, MI: William B Eerdmanns Publishing Co. 1983) 521.

[4] Fasching and Dechant, *Comparative Religious Ethics.* p. 98-102.

[5] Humberto R. Maturana and Bernard Poerksen, *From Being to Doing: the Origins of a Biology of Cognition* translated by Wolfram Karl Koeck and Alison Rosemary Koeck (Heidelberg, Germany: Carl-Auer Verlag, 2004) p. 206-208.

[6] Bonhoeffer, p. 17.

[7] Dussell, p. 50. Italics mine.

[8] Harold Flender, *Rescue in Denmark* (New York: MacFadden Books, 1964) p. 28, 29.

[9] Arendt, p. 172

[10] As quoted, Flender, p. 16.

[11] Arendt, p. 172.

[12] Allan A. Boesak, *Comfort and Protest: The Apocalypse from a South African Perspective* (Philadelphia: Westminster Press, 1987) p. 24.

[13] Clearly many other interpreters interpret this parable morally. Matthew himself does. In Matthew 13: 37-43, Matthew interprets this "parable" in the following way: "The one who sows the good seed is the Son of Man; the field is the world and the good seed are the children of the kingdom; the weeds are the children of the evil one, and the enemy who sowed them is the devil; the harvest is the end of the age and the reapers are angels, and they will collect out of his kingdom all causes of sin and all evildoers, and they will throw them into the furnace of fire where there will be weeping and gnashing of teeth. Then the righteous will shine like the sun in the kingdom of their Father." The trouble with Matthew's interpretation of Jesus' parable is that Matthew converts Jesus' parable into an allegory. An allegory is a story where every element in the story has a corresponding and definite referent in a world outside the story. The allegorizing of a parable is always in the interest of the dominator system because it creates one and only one possible interpretation of the story. A parable allows for many possible interpretations. For a further discussion of this common mistake that even the Biblical writers made in efforts to interpret parables see Gustafson, *Biblical Amnesia* p. 88-94.

[14] Bauman, *Modernity and the Holocaust.* p. 91, 92.

[15] Martin Hengel, *Crucifixion in the Ancient World and the Folly of the Message of the Cross* (Phildelphia: Fortress Press, 1977) p. 33.

[16] Ibid, p. 34.

[17] Ibid, p. 51.

[18] Juvenal 6: 219ff. As quoted, Hengel, p. 57, 58.

[19] Ernst Käsemann, *Perspectives on Paul,* translated by Margaret Kohl (Phildelphia: Fortress Press, 1971) p. 36.

[20] Martin Luther, *Lectures on Galatians, 1535, "* translated by Jaroslav Pelikan in *Luther's Works,* Vol. 26 (St. Louis: Concordia Publishing House, 1963) p. 277. Italics mine.

[21] The word "Law" here is problematic. Paul writes in Greek. He uses the word *NOMOS* which translates as law in the Bible. The "Law" to which Paul refers, however, is not some jurisdictional code. It is the *Torah.* The *Torah* is the first five books of the Hebrew Bible which, along with the writing of the prophets, was the only sacred book in existence for Jews and Christians at the time Paul wrote. Unfortunately, we normally do not think *Torah* when we here the word law. We think of the 10 commandments which are contained in the *Torah* but are not the entire *Torah.* This is not so problematic in the instance discussed above, however, it becomes quite interesting when Paul discusses the law in terms of letter and spirit. It is the spirit that gives life, and it is the letter that kills. Paul is arguing against literalist interpretations of Scripture. The fact that Paul does it in the Christian Bible itself, ought to worry a literalist Christian.

[22] There are many people of good will in the world, but people of good will who are within the dominator system still perform acts that are death-dealing. Often, they do so with the best of intentions. This is largely because they have uncritically accepted the worldview of the dominator system. George E. Tinker, *Missionary Conquest* discusses the efforts of missionaries like John Eliot, Junipero Serra, Pierre-Jean De Smet and Henry Benjamin Whipple. He summarized his well argued and well documented theme in the following way. "What I call cultural genocide functions at times as conscious intent, but at other times at such a systemic level that it may be largely subliminal. In such cases, the good intent of some may be so mired in unrecognized systemic structures that they even remain unaware of the destruction that results from those good intentions." p. 5.

[23] It is of vital importance to note that Paul's argument is an argument internal to the dominator system. It does not pertain to those who have always opposed the dominator system from the outside such as Native Americans and others who formed their cultures prior to contact with civilization.

[24] Zygmunt Bauman, *Postmodern Ethics* (Malden, MA: Blackwell, 1993) p. 9.

[25] Ibid, p. 10-15.

[26] Emmanuel Levinas, *Ethics and Infinity*, translated by Richard A. Cohen (Pittsburgh: Duquesne University Press, 1985) p. 95-101.

[27] Bauman, *Postmodern Ethics*, p. 85-88.

[28] Ibid, 88-92.

[29] Levinas, p. 77.

[30] Actually, the Good Samaritan story is admittedly a story. The people in it may not have existed much less their reasoning processes. But as is true of most stories, they may give us an indication of our own thoughts and feelings even when the story does not explicitly state them.

[31] It is not that the dominator system did not exist in the Americas. The Mayans, the Aztecs, perhaps the Incas and others had their agricultural revolutions. Like the agricultural revolutions of the Euro-Asian (including Egypt) land mass, these populations developed morality and built their pyramids and social hierarchies. The difference between the American Indian version of the dominator system and the Euro-Asian version is that the Euro-Asian version did not allow an alternative to the dominator system. The oppressed people of the Euro-Asian version of the dominator system would strike, revolt, force the system to formulate new programs, but they would never just quit. They never would just walk away. Daniel Quinn's book *Beyond Civilization*, p. 29-54, speculates that the American Indian version of the dominator system was not able to instill this attitude completely. From time to time, a good number of the oppressed would just walk away. This, Quinn says, explains why anthropologists have been unable to explain the mysterious

demise of many very highly developed civilizations of Pre-Columbian America like the Mayans and Anasazi. These anthropologists cannot conceive of people simply abandoning civilization for any reason. Quinn says that no one in the Euro-Asian version of the dominator system ever just walked away. He is wrong. The Bible records one group walking away from one of the most highly developed civilizations known to humanity – Egypt. The Bible itself might be read in terms of the fact that the Hebrews just walked away from the dominator system of Egypt. My book, *Biblical Amnesia,* was an attempt to read the Bible in this manner.

[32] Deloria, p. 87.

[33] Tinker, *Spirit and Resistance,* p. 63-65.

[34] This quotation is originally from Jedidiah Morse, "A Report to the Secretary of War on Indian Affairs" (Washington, D.C.: U.S. Government Printing Office, 1822) p. 207 cited from Louis Burns, *A History of the Osage People* (Fallbrook, CA: Ciga Press, 1989) p. 289-290 as quoted Ibid, p. ix,x.

[35] Harvey Arden, *Noble Red Man: Lakota Wisdomkeeper Matthew King* (Hillsbora, OR: Beyond Worlds Publishing, 1994) p. 82. As quoted, Glenn T. Morris, "Resistance, Politics, Colonization and the Law," in *Native Voices: American Indian Identity and Resistance,* edited by Richard A. Grounds, George E. Tinker and David E Wilkins (Lawrence, KA: University of Kansas Press, 2003) p. 97.

[36] Luther Standing Bear, *Land of the Spotted Eagle* (Boston: Houghton Mifflin, 1938) as quoted Deloria, p.90.

[37] Tinker, *Spirit and Resistance,* p. 15.

[38] Ibid.

[39] Richard Erdoes and Alfonso Ortiz, *American Myths and Legends* (New York: Pantheon, 1984) p. 62-65 in Tinker, *Spirit and Resistance,* p. 16, 17.

[40] Walter Wink, *Engaging the Powers: Discernment and Resistance in a World of Domination* (Minneapolis, MN: Fortress, 1992) p. 12-30.

[41] Ibid, p. 18.

Chapter 6: Ethical Virtues

[1] Elie Wiesel, *The Forgotten* (New York: Schocken Books, 1992) p. 36.

[2] Alasdair MacIntyre, *After Virtue: A Study in Moral Theory,* 2nd Edition (Notre Dame, IN: University of Notre Dame Press, 1984) p. 191.

[3] Ibid, p. 191,192.

[4] Ibid, p. 192, 193.

[5] Bernard Loomer, "Two Kinds of Power," *Criterion,* 15, no.1 (Winter, 1976) p. 14.

[6] See Howard Zinn, *A People's History of the United States: 1492 – Present* and Howard Zinn and Anthony Arnove, *Voices of a People's*

History of the United States (New York: Seven Stories Press, 2004) to begin to understand that, in the dominator system, rights are never merely given. They are always won. They are won when a group of people obtains enough unilateral power to force the powers that be to grant concessions.

[7] Peter Paris, *Social Teachings of the Black Churches* (Philadelphia: Fortress Press, 1985) p. 114.

[8] Ibid, p. 115.

[9] Ibid, p. 118.

[10] Ibid, p. 118, italics mine.

[11] Walter Brueggemann, *Genesis: Interpretation A Biblical Commentary for Teaching and Preaching* (Atlanta, GA: John Knox Press, 1982) p. 168.

[12] Ibid, p. 168-172.

[13] Brevard Childs, *The Book of Exodus: An Old Testament Library* (Philadelphia: Westminister Press, 1974) p. 567 ff.

[14] Ibid.

[15] Douglas John Hall, *Lighten Our Darkness: Toward an Indigenous Theology of the Cross* (Philadelphia: Westminster Press, 1976) p. 93-100.

[16] The Harvard Working Group on New and Resurgent Diseases, "Globalization, Development and the Spread of Disease," *The Case Against the Global Economy*, edited by Jerry Mander and Edward Goldsmith (San Francisco: Sierra Club Book, 1996) p. 164.

[17] Walter Brueggemann, *David's Truth: In Israel's Imagination and Memory* (Philadelphia: Fortress Press, 1986) p. 55-65.

[18] Ibid, p. 56.

[19] Ibid, p. 60.

[20] Claus Westermann, *Creation* translated by John J. Scullion, SJ (Philadelphia: Fortress Press, 1974) p. 61.

[21] Exodus 20. There are other, slightly different versions of the Ten Commandments. See Deuteronomy 5 for example.

[22] Deloria, p. 257-270.

[23] Robert Jenson, *A Large Catechism* (Delhi, NY: American Lutheran Publicity Bureau, 1991) p. 11.

Chapter 7: Beyond What We Are

[1] E. F. Schumacher, *Good Work* (New York: Harper Colophon Books, 1979) p. 32

[2] Kirkpatrick Sale, "Principles of Bioregionalism," *The Case Against the Global Economy,* p. 471-484.

[3] Fasching and Delchant, *Comparative Religious Ethics*, p. 16, 17.

[4] Popper, *Open Society and Its Enemies,* Vol. I. p. 132.

[5] Thomas Cahill, *How the Irish Saved Civilization: the Untold Story of Ireland's Heroic Role from the Fall of Rome to the Rise of Medieval Europe* (New York: Doubleday, 1995) p 114.

[6] Diamond, *Guns Germs and Steal*

[7] Peter N. Gillingham, "The Making of Good Work," in Schumacher, *Good Work*, pp. 147-217.

[8] Ibid, p. 155.

[9] Ibid, p. 160.

[10] Robert G. O'Meally, "Blues for Huckleberry," in Mark Twain, *Adventures of Huckleberry Finn,* (New York: Barnes and Noble Classic, 2003) p. xxxvii.

[11] Twain, pp. 193-195.

[12] Ibid, p. 263.

[13] George M. Fredrickson, *Racism,* p. 128.

[14] Gunnar Myrdal, *An American Dilemma* (New York: 1944) p. 997, lxi. As quoted, Ibid, p. 129

[15] Ibid, p. 132.

[16] Hannah Arendt, *The Origins of Totalitarianism,* p. viii.